Abundant Sonshine

Devotions to Entertain, Enlighten and Educate

Cynthia Irish Hockins

ISBN: 1547273739
ISBN 13: 9781547273737

This book is dedicated to my late husband Dick with my thanks for 46 wonderful years. He always felt I had a book in me somewhere; and also to my children – Linda Evans and Rich Hockins – who have inspired me and taught me so much over the years.

My FIRST THANKS for *Abundant Sonshine* definitely go to God. Years ago I felt the pull to join a Bible study group but my "busy schedule" could not make the time. In His infinite wisdom, God moved my family 375 miles to a new city and state and the first thing I was invited to join was a Bible Study. The next five years were spent in an in-depth study program that changed my life and rearranged my priorities. Initially I was shocked to see other women actually *writing* in their Bibles during the lectures and discussions, but I soon began underlining, highlighting and occasionally even dating verses and passages that "spoke to me" in one way or another. (I highly recommend this practice!) I began note-taking and annotating, and then categorizing and alphabetizing my thoughts and topics, and eventually expanding on them with more research leading to short devotions.

Additional thanks go to the following for their encouraging words, their listening ears and their open hearts:

...my daughter Linda who repeatedly said, "Of <u>course</u> you can, Mom! Just do it!"

...my sister Diana for her helpful suggestions and her patience;

...my wonderful Mom, now in heaven, who often said, "Don't just think it! Write it down!"

...my Christian sisters wherever I have lived who continue to influence and encourage me.

Index

Angels

Bless them! They are always up in the air harping on something!

THE DICTIONARY SAYS an angel is a messenger – a supernatural being, either a good one or a bad one – usually with more than human power, intelligence, etc. It can be a guiding spirit or a conventionalized image of a figure in human form with wings and a halo. We tend to think of angels as being beautiful and good. Angels can render many services. In Biblical times they guarded Paradise after Adam and Eve were expelled from the Garden of Eden. They ministered to Jesus after His temptation. An angel strengthened Jesus when He prayed in Gethsemane before His arrest – and an angel told His followers of the resurrection after the crucifixion. We're told in Revelations that on the last day angels will harvest souls to prepare for God's judgment.

A Bible concordance says that an angel appeared to at least 13 people in the Old Testament and then in Judges 2:1-4, an angel appeared to all Israel. In the New Testament there are many specific instances given, including the announcement of Jesus' conception in Matthew and an angel heralding his birth in Luke. An angel also appeared to "shepherds" and to "certain women," and their appearance is noted in seven churches in Revelations.

Overall, the Bible cites many kinds of angels, but right now let's focus on the "good angels." Genesis tells us that angels guide. Psalm 34 says they surround and protect. Daniel 6 and Acts 12:7-10 says they deliver. In Acts we read that an angel of the Lord appeared to Peter in his jail cell saying he would be released. These angels passed the guards to reach Peter, and then left the prison unnoticed. Matthew 24:31 says they <u>gather</u>. Acts 27:23 & 24 say that they <u>comfort.</u> Paul told of an angel of God visiting him and telling him not to be afraid as he was tried before Caesar. This same angel predicted that his ship would be lost but said no person ON it would be lost.

Angels come into our lives in many forms today. They may not always have wings and halos outwardly, but many of us have experienced a friend or a stranger coming unexpectedly into our lives at a time of need. It may have been to offer comfort, or lend a helping hand, or to prepare or share a meal, or just to offer a shoulder to lean on or an ear that is willing to listen. Sometimes these angels just sit quietly and we are comforted by their presence.

We never know when we might be led to act as an angel – or exactly when we might need an angel. Be thankful that our loving, kind Heavenly Father is looking out for our best interests. He wants us to be aware of others in need and then to be grateful when WE are the recipients of one of His special, ministering angels.

When the Son of Man comes in his glory, and all the angels
with him, he will sit on his throne in heavenly glory.
Matthew 25:31

Patience

—— § ——

Patience is truly a virtue – and it is one that carries a lot of "wait."

JAMES 5:7-8 TELL us that patient waiting is often the highest way of doing God's will. In describing patience, my dictionary gives several words and examples for patience, and one of them is perseverance. Earlier in the Book of James, in chapter 1, he says: *"Consider it pure joy, my brothers, whenever you face trials of many kinds, because you know that the testing of your faith develops perseverance."*

Someone once said that patience is idling your motor when you'd rather be stripping your gears. Though we do not always understand the purpose of waiting for something, God asks us to trust Him to know the best time and place for all things. Many of the things for which I am most grateful are those times when God did NOT answer a prayer in the way I had asked that it be answered. He knew all too well that my petition was not the right one, and he chose to teach me patience as he showed me HIS way and that HIS answer was the best one.

A Bible Study leader once cautioned the class about praying for patience. Her reason was that you can only learn patience when you are confronted with a situation that would usually make you impatient. God does not GIVE us patience. Nor is patience a gift! Instead God gives us opportunities to LEARN patience. I think of patience as a fruit. A fruit must grow and ripen in order to be ready in its time.

The writer William Barclay explained patience this way: *"The Greek word for patience literally means endurance. It is more than patient submissiveness. There is a note of triumph! It is the ability to bear things in such a triumphant way that it transfigures them. It enables a man to pass the breaking point and not to break, and always to greet the unseen with a cheer."*

Verses 1-3 of Psalm 37 have some beautiful thoughts on this subject. *"Do not fret because of evil men or be envious of those who do wrong; for like the grass they will soon wither, like green plants they will soon die away. Trust in the Lord and do good; dwell in the land and enjoy safe pasture."* This means that when life takes a detour and does not go as we expect, it is important to remember God has not abandoned or deserted us. He always desires the best for us and sometimes that involves waiting.

Remember - patient waiting is often the highest method of doing God's will!

*"Delight yourself in the Lord and he will
give you the desires of your heart.
Commit your way to the Lord; trust in him and he will do this:
He will make your righteousness shine like the dawn,
the justice of your cause like the noonday sun.
Be still before the Lord and wait patiently for him."*
Psalm 37:4-7

Grace

— ∮ —

IN ADDITION TO the word "grace" being a feminine name – and that was my maternal grandmother's name – my dictionary has a long paragraph devoted to definitions of the word "grace." Here are some of those definitions:

1. Beauty or charm of form, movement or expression.
2. An attractive quality, feature, or manner, etc.
3. A sense of what is right and proper, decency – thoughtfulness.
4. Good will; favor.
5. A short prayer of blessing or thanks for a meal.
6. A title of respect in speaking to or of an archbishop, duke or duchess.
7. Musically it says ornamental notes or effects, collectively.
8. The merited love and favor of God toward man.
9. The divine influence acting in man to make him pure and good.
10. A special virtue given to a person by God.

I've often heard it said that grace means unmerited favor. The dictionary says merit is something deserving a reward. We receive God's grace without ever actually doing anything for it. It is a **gift** from God. Another way to say it is *"Grace is EVERYthing for NOTHing for those who don't actually deserve ANYthing."* God's grace means that he forgives us unconditionally. He forgives us for our limitations, and for our sins, both deliberate and accidental.

When you visit a jeweler and ask to see a diamond or precious stone, in or out of a setting, the first thing the jeweler usually does is spread out a black cloth to display it so the diamond or stone will appear brighter against that

5

dark background. We could say that this is like God's <u>grace</u> shining brightly for us.

It's been said that grace is the most important word in the Bible and that it is the heart of the Gospel. Grace does not depend on what we have done for God, but rather on what God has done for us. In II Corinthians 9:8 & 9 it says: *"And God is able to make all grace abound to you, so that in <u>all</u> things at <u>all</u> times, having <u>all</u> that you need, you will abound in every good work. It is written: 'He has scattered abroad his gifts to the poor; his righteousness endures forever.'"*

In Galatians 2:20-21 Paul says this: *"The life I live in the body, I live by faith in the Son of God, who loved me and gave himself for me. I do not set aside the grace of God, for if righteousness could be gained through the law, Christ died for nothing."* Paul was constantly aware of God's grace in his life. In total love he tried to live up to God's will for him in making these truths known to all who would listen.

If we seek God's will for our lives, and then attempt to live up to God's standards, we will be very aware of God's grace as a true part of our lives. So I close in peace and I wish each of us the continuing grace of God.

But by the grace of God I am what I am, and
his grace to me was not without effect.
No, I worked harder than all of them — yet not I,
but the grace of God that was with me.
I Corinthians 15:10

Safe and Safety

———— § ————

THERE ARE MANY definitions given in the dictionary for the words safe and safety, and these definitions are very similar, but the main explanations say that to be safe is to be free from danger or from damage – to be secure, or to feel secure. The Bible Concordance says it is living without fear or harm.

I noticed there were many phrases that followed safe and safety in the dictionary. Things like safeguard and safety glass, safety pin and safety valve. Safety glass is shatterproof which is accomplished by putting 2 pieces of glass together with a transparent, plastic substance between them. A safety pin will hold 2 things together, often temporarily until you can get to a needle and thread for a permanent fix. A safety valve is an automatic valve for a steam boiler and it will release steam if the pressure gets too great. A safety valve is also described as "any outlet for emotion, energy, etc." A safety net is designed to catch a person who may fall in the course of fulfilling his duties or responsibilities.

There are also a number of references to safety in the Book of Psalms. The first one that comes to mind is found in Psalm 4 verse 8 where it says: *"I will lie down and sleep in peace, for you alone, O Lord, make me dwell in safety."* In Psalm 16, the very first verse, David says, *"Keep me safe, O God, for in you I take refuge."*

One of the greatest examples in the Bible of safety or security under severe strain would be Daniel in the Old Testament when he was thrust into the den of lions. After he was falsely accused and put into the den as a punishment, a stone was rolled across the door and King Darius sealed it with his own signet so no one could rescue Daniel. But the next morning, when King Darius went to the den, Daniel cried out to him and said God had sent an angel to close the lions' mouths and they did not hurt him. Daniel was truly a trusting man! Not only that, but King Darius made a decree to all in his royal dominion that the God of Daniel was a living god whose kingdom shall never be destroyed. He said Daniel's God not only delivers and rescues, He works signs and wonders in heaven and on earth and he acknowledged that God had saved Daniel from the power of the lions. To that I would send up a loud Amen!

In Chapter 33 of Deuteronomy, Moses blesses each of the tribes of Israel and he finishes in verse 28 by saying, *"So Israel will live in safety alone; Jacob's spring is secure in a land of grain and new wine, where the heavens drop dew."*

In the King James Version of the Bible, Zechariah 14 verse 11 reads*: "And men shall dwell in it (the City of Jerusalem), and there shall be no more utter destruction; but Jerusalem shall be safely inhabited."*

Although neither the dictionary nor the Concordance make direct comparisons of these two words to Jesus and His impact on our lives, He truly does provide us with a very secure feeling once we acknowledge Him as our Lord and Savior. He is our safe harbor in a storm. He is our safeguard against Satan who continually tries to worm his way into our lives. He is our safety glass with God in the middle and Jesus and the Holy Spirit pressed together with Him to help us keep our lives shatterproof. He is the safety valve that helps us hold our anger in check when necessary and the One we can turn to for the energy and the will to go on in times of severe trial. He is our safety pin because we adhere – or pin – ourselves to Him once we call Him into our lives, and we are held together by His love and the strength and fulfillment of His beautiful promises. He is our safety net when we stumble and fall. The strength of His net keeps us from harm and it catches us and helps us get back on our feet and start over again.

Memorize these verses and carry them with you for your own personal safety: Psalm 147:5-7, *"Great is our Lord and mighty in power; his understanding has no limit. The Lord sustains the humble but casts the wicked to the ground. Sing to the Lord with thanksgiving."*

Refuge

————— § —————

A REFUGE IS said to be a place of protection – a shelter from danger – a place of safety for anyone or anything that fears for its life or well-being. An example of a refuge might be an area designated as a National Wildlife Refuge area. This Refuge System is managed by the U.S. Fish & Wildlife Services who see to the conservation of America's fish, wildlife and plants. Their mission is to manage a network of lands and waters for the conservation, management and where appropriate, restoration of fish, wildlife and plant resources and their habitat. The first such refuge was designated by Theodore Roosevelt in 1903 and it is at Pelican Island, Florida near the town of Vero Beach. The System has grown since then and it now encompasses more than 150 million acres and includes 552 national wildlife refuges plus 37 wetland management districts. These Refuges are home to more than 700 species of birds, 220 species of mammals, 250 reptile and amphibian species and more than 200 species of fish. Without these designated areas, many of these birds, animals, fish & wildlife of all sorts would now be extinct. (Indiana boasts 3 such refuge locations, all located in the southern part of the state.)

God could be said to be our personal refuge. When we focus on Him, He becomes our place of protection – our shelter from danger – and a place of safety from anything that would seek to point our lives in a different direction. His mission is to keep us in His Word, to help us live by His commandments and the tenets He has laid out for us, particularly those listed in the Bible.

The Book of Psalms is filled with many beautiful references to God as our personal refuge. In Psalm 5:11 David wrote, *"But let all who take refuge in you be glad; let them sing for joy."* In Psalm 9:9 he went on to say, *"The Lord is a refuge for the oppressed, a stronghold in times of trouble."*

Later, in Psalm 16, David is talking directly to the Lord when he says, *"Keep me safe, O God, for in you I take refuge."* He is acknowledging his need for safety and protection, and he is saying God is his safe retreat. In that retreat he realizes he is safe from any kind of danger and no harm will befall him. In Psalm 18 David refers to God as a shield for all who would take refuge in him. Psalm 31 calls him a rock of refuge and later in that Psalm he says, *"How great is your goodness, which you have stored up for those who fear you – for those who take refuge in you."* In Psalm 34 he says the man is blessed who takes refuge in the Lord. Later, in Psalm 59 David says his strength comes from the Lord because He is a refuge in times of trouble.

In the latter part of David's life, in his old age, he realizes enemies are threatening him because his physical strength is waning and he asks the Lord to rescue him and to be his rock of refuge and his deliverer. Psalm 91 verse 4 is one of my favorites. It says this: *"He will cover you with his feathers, and under his wings you will find refuge; his faithfulness will be your shield and rampart."* Doesn't that paint a beautiful picture for us?

In closing, these verses from Psalm 145 speak volumes. Verses 13 & 14 say this: *"The Lord is faithful to all his promises and loving toward all he has made. The Lord upholds all those who fall and lifts up all who are bowed down."* Later in verses 18 & 19 David says, *"The Lord is near to all who call on him and he fulfills the desires of those who fear him; he hears their cry and saves them. The Lord watches over all who love him."* Listen to Him – call on Him – and may you find your own personal refuge is in His loving arms and under His protective wings.

God is our refuge and strength, an ever present help in trouble.
Therefore we will not fear, though the earth give way and the mountains
fall into the heart of the sea.
Psalm 46:1, 2

Opening Day

This morning starts a new day in my life, Lord.
Let this day be one of opening...
Let me open my arms for surprise hugs.
Help my eyes to be open to special needs around me.
Open my heart to one needing a shoulder, or an ear.
Open my heart, my eyes, my soul, and myself to You
so I may close my day
Knowing You and I spent it together.

Shepherd

—— § ——

ONE OF MY favorite Sundays in the church year is Shepherd Sunday. I look forward to hearing the lessons and thinking about Jesus as our Shepherd, and I like the references to all of us being one of His flock. The dictionary says a shepherd is one who herds sheep, or one who leads, such as a clergyman. A concordance describes the duties of a shepherd toward his flock and gives Biblical references for each. He is to: defend, water, give rest to, to know, number, secure pasture for, and search for the lost.

The Bible makes many references to Jesus as a Shepherd. There are several in Ezekiel. Chapter 34:12 says, *"As a shepherd seeks out his flock, so will I seek out my sheep."* A couple verses later it says, *"I will feed My flock and I will cause them to lie down"...* and the next verse says, *"I will seek that which was lost."* In Isaiah 40:11 it says *"He shall feed his flock like a shepherd."*

A good portion of John, Chapter 10, is devoted to the shepherd and his flock. He refers to Himself as the gate through which the sheep may enter the pen – and whoever enters through this gate will be saved. In verse 14 He says, *"I am the good shepherd. The good shepherd lays down His life for the sheep,"* and He goes on to say, *"He calls his own sheep by name and leads them out. They follow for they know his voice,"* and He says, *"I have come that they may have life and have it to the full."* in John 10:10.

Jesus is referred to as the <u>good</u> shepherd in John 10. He is the <u>chief</u> shepherd in I Peter. He is the <u>great</u> shepherd in Hebrews 13. He is the <u>one</u> shepherd in John 10. He is the <u>gentle</u> shepherd in Isaiah 40. In Matthew 25:34

there is a reference to Jesus separating the sheep and the goats. The sheep will be on his right and he will say to them, *"Come, you who are blessed by my Father, take your inheritance, the kingdom prepared for you since the creation of the world...."*

Now let's think about the sheep! The dictionary's definition of sheep says it is a cud-chewing mammal related to goats, with heavy wool and edible flesh called mutton. It also says it refers to one who is meek, timid and submissive.

During my research, I learned that sheep are really very stupid creatures and they can be incredibly stubborn. They have an offensive odor and they are not only prone to sickness, they are also very susceptible to parasites and diseases. They can be extremely helpless and they are very fearful creatures as well. They are known to be destructive of land and its resources and they are often harsh and hardheaded with each other. They have a predilection to wander, and they are easy prey for predators. No other class of livestock demands so much constant, endless attention and meticulous care. And Jesus called us his sheep! In some ways it's not very flattering, is it? Especially when we are being compared to sheep with Jesus as our Shepherd and caretaker! But if we look further, we will see that first, sheep are very innocent animals. Second, they are useful in every way from their wool to their milk and to their meat. Third, John 1:29 refers to sheep as sacrifices. Fourth, sheep are said to know their master's voice. So let's see – that's humble, useful, innocent, know their master -- -- shouldn't that describe us?

A sheep's wool is highly prized, but not necessarily in its original state. In its natural state, after shearing takes place, raw wool is not shiny and snowy white. It is actually dark, dirty, stained with mud and manure, and full of tics, burrs & mites. It is also greasy and oily with lanolin which, when hot, emits a most disagreeable and repulsive odor. Only after the wool has been removed from the sheep, washed and cleansed, does it become attractive and useful. This, too, could describe our Christian walk.

We start out as the wool, not shiny and snowy white, but dirty and stained by sin. It is only after we submit ourselves and our lives to Christ that we are washed and cleansed, and then we become useful Christians.

Jesus knew all of the undesirable qualities of sheep and he still loved them all! They did not repel him or repulse him. He loved them for what they were and for what they could become. As the <u>Good</u> Shepherd, Christ laid down his life for the sheep. As the <u>Great</u> Shepherd, He leads and feeds his sheep. As the <u>Chief</u> Shepherd, He will come again as King of Kings and Lord of Lords.

Try reading the 23rd Psalm slowly, verse by verse, and think about each verse as you read it. Focus on what David is telling us through each phrase. *The Lord is my shepherd; I shall not want. He makes me lie down in green pastures, he leads me beside still waters, He restores my soul. He guides me in paths of righteousness for his name's sake. Yea, though I walk through the valley of the shadow of death, I will fear no evil, for you are with me. Your rod and your staff, they comfort me. You prepare a table before me in the presence of my enemies. You anoint my head with oil; my cup overflows. Surely goodness and mercy will follow me all the days of my life, and I will dwell in the house of the Lord forever.*

I was reminded of some important things in reading this Psalm and doing research on sheep. I learned that sheep will not lie down unless they are free of all fear. Nor will they lie down unless they are free from friction with others of their kind. They will not lie down unless they are free of pests like flies or parasites because they cannot relax. They will not lie down as long as they feel in need of finding food. So for David to say He makes me lie down in green pastures, he is saying he is <u>not</u> afraid, he has <u>no</u> quarrels with anyone, he is <u>not</u> aggravated or distracted, and he is <u>not</u> hungry. In other words, God has taken care of it all! And then there is the phrase about walking through the valley of the shadow of death. Please note that it says <u>through</u> this valley. Sometimes we may feel like we are

<u>in</u> the valley of the shadow of death, but these words say we are walking <u>through</u> it – not dwelling there. During our lifetime we may have many "mountaintop experiences" but it is often in the valley experiences that we come closer to God and feel his presence.

The writer of Hebrews sums it up nicely in Hebrews 13:20 when he says:

May the God of peace, who through the blood of the eternal covenant
brought back from the dead our Lord Jesus,
that great Shepherd of the sheep,
equip you with everything good for doing his will,
and may he work in us what is pleasing to him,
through Jesus Christ, in whom be glory for ever and ever. Amen.

Seasons

———— § ————

HAVE YOU EVER thought of the stages of our lives in relation to the seasons of the year or to a twelve-month calendar? In Genesis Chapter 8 verse 22, following the flood, God said, *"As long as the earth endures, seedtime and harvest, cold and heat, summer and winter, day and night will never cease."*

These verses sound like the springtime – a time of joy – a time of renewal and rebirth. Solomon says spring is a season of singing. Flowers push up out of the ground. Buds and leaves burst forth on trees, bushes and shrubs and the grasses turn green after the cold, dormancy of winter. Also at this time, many birds will return to thrive and multiply in areas that only recently were experiencing cold temperatures and were covered with snow and slush. This part of the calendar year could also equate to <u>our</u> birth when we came forth from our mother's wombs. In the springtime of our lives we also sprouted and grew as we settled into our new surroundings. We push forth to enter this world and this is called birth. Later in this spring of our lives we begin to learn about God and His love for us, and we learn that He has specific plans for each of us and we are here for a reason.

Summer is a time to kick back, relax and take life easy. It is often a time for travel and vacations and a time for family reunions and the renewing of old friendships. We relax and we grow and mature through the summer of our lives.

After summer we come to autumn or fall, or harvest time. Plantings have reached full growth and are now ready for harvesting. We mature and reach our full physical growth at this time. For many of us, it is during this time that we find our lives melding with other lives and new family units are formed. Temperatures are pleasant at the beginning of the fall season, and then ever so slowly the temperatures begin to wane. We see the leaves changing their colors and then they slowly fall away from the trees.

So spring is a season of joy – summer is a season of renewing – fall is a season of change – and then we come to wintertime, this last season of our lifetime. Winter is a time of settling down, a time for turning our thoughts inward and also upward. Plants and animals hibernate to stave off the cold. We humans bundle up in warmer clothing and we often spend more time in the warmth and familiarity of our own comfortable surroundings.

When we came into this world, we entered crying and all of those around us were happy. They smiled and laughed as they welcomed us and cradled us in their arms. As Christians, let's go OUT of this life smiling as those around us cry for joy that we are going to be with the One who made all seasons. We are going to be welcomed and cradled in the loving arms of the One who is our Lord and Savior and Father of us all.

The winter is past; the rains are over and
gone. Flowers appear on the earth;
the season of singing has come; the cooing of doves is heard in our land.
The fig tree forms its early fruit; the blossom-
ing vines spread their fragrance.
Song of Songs 2:11, 12

Feet

———— § ————

EARLY IN THE Book of Proverbs we are told that the Lord hates sinners and He warns that their feet rush into sin and they have no moral direction. Later, in the 6th chapter, there is a list of many things the Lord hates and finds detestable and these include a heart that devises wicked schemes and feet that rush into evil.

In the New Testament; we often find the feet of Jesus to be busy, and more often than not, they were on the move. They were seldom still. His feet took Him from place to place as He continued about His mission. These feet of Jesus also served in many ways. They walked into the Jordan River to be baptized by John and thus began his life of ministry. They walked into the wedding at Cana where he performed the first of His many miracles, this time turning water into wine. They walked from town to town spreading His good news that forgiveness, salvation and eternal life were available to all. He washed the feet of His disciples in a gesture of humility and love – and He later told them to go place to place, town to town, shaking the dust off their feet as they went. Then these same beautiful feet of Jesus were cruelly nailed to a cross as He was crucified.

Today, our feet can walk – they can trip – they can stumble – they can step and be stepped ON – they can take right steps or wrong steps – they can dance to show joy and they can shuffle when we are weary. But remember, they can also serve. Psalm 119 tells us that God's Word is a lamp unto our feet – a light for our path.

May each of us remember that when we stumble or trip, God is there. He is holding out His hands, ready to catch us or to pick us up, willing to hold us and steady us, and then to help us step out and move on. Let's strive for happy feet and add them to our helping hands as we live in His will for our lives.

Then Miriam the prophetess, Aaron's
(& Moses') sister, took a tambourine
in her hand, and all the women followed her, with tambourines
and dancing. Miriam sang to them, "Sing to the Lord,
for he is highly exalted."
Exodus 15:20-21

Self-Control

THE LAST FRUIT of the spirit listed in Galatians Chapter 5 is self-control. Because it is listed last does not make this "fruit" any less important than all the others. It may be the last to make the list, but it carries a lot of weight and a great deal of challenge for us. If we are to be in charge of our personal self-control, we must learn first that we are not competing with anyone else, only ourselves. Solomon wrote in Proverbs 16, the Living Bible version, that it is better to have self-control than to control an army.

Self-control can mean many different things as we go through life. As youngsters, we are encouraged to use self-control with our speech and not talk back or sass our parents or teachers, etc., and not use language that others might find offensive. We are told to use our self-control and not use any form of physical abuse to get along with our siblings, our classmates or our friends when they don't automatically agree with us.

As adults, if we can develop and encourage the fruit of self-control, it will in turn help the fruit of our character by expanding it and helping it grow. William Barclay, an English theologian, once said this: *"Self-control is the virtue which enables a person to master his own life so that he is able to be the servant of others."*

Although the phrase self-control is not used, Proverbs 31 verses 10 to 30 describe a wise woman and a wife of noble character. These verses imply a great deal of self-control as this wise character willingly goes about her household and family duties in a spirit of love and devotion.

For the Christian in today's world, self-control means we acknowledge Christ as being in control of us and our lives – the physical and emotional parts as well as the moral part. We are to feel that the basis for our whole being is God's to do with as He chooses.

Many words can be used to describe a state of self-control. It is the control of one's emotions, desires and actions; control of one's self. We are to curb or restrain our feelings so that self-control reigns us in and causes us to think twice before taking an action that may be hurtful or harmful or even illegal. We are to have self-control and authority over ourselves and our emotions at all times.

To enjoy a really good taste in your mouth, sample and enjoy the true self-respect that accompanies true self-control.

"For God did not give us a spirit of timidity but a
spirit of power and love and self-control.
II Timothy 1:7

Bridge
A Link-to-the-Lord

—— § ——

WEBSTER'S DICTIONARY DEFINES a bridge as "A structure erected over a depression or an obstacle, as over a river." When there is an area to be spanned, engineers measure and sketch plans called blueprints. When the time comes to execute these plans, the workers start the construction on both sides of this area. Work always begins on solid ground. Stakes, often called pilings, are driven into the earth to carry the vertical load. They act as supports for the structure and now pieces can be added horizontally, one piece at a time. A line is cast from one side of the opening to the other so it is secured on both sides. This guideline assures that the two extensions will meet in the middle.

As I considered these facts, I couldn't help but compare bridge building to my relationship with God through Jesus Christ. I am on one side of the River of Life and God is on the other. By accepting Jesus Christ as my Lord and Savior, I am establishing myself on solid ground. This commitment could be called my "piling." My guideline is Jesus Christ! He acts as my invisible support line and my connection to God by focusing my thoughts and actions in the proper direction. As I read His Word and acquire more knowledge of Him, and as I follow His plan for my life, I am adding sections to my bridge. If I attempt to add a section that is out of kilter with His plan, He immediately pulls on His end of the guideline to realign and redirect me.

We each have the opportunity of connecting ourselves and heading in the right direction to establish our personal bridge. God is always there reaching out and casting lines. In sharing my love and knowledge of Jesus daily I just may be encouraging someone else to lay out a blueprint, establish a foundation, and begin the construction of his own personal bridge.

What a beautiful picture this creates as we picture millions and millions of invisible lines reaching and stretching upward, knowing that each one represents a direct link to the Lord!

Let us then approach the throne of grace with confidence,
so that we may receive mercy and find grace
to help us in our time of need.
Hebrews 4:16

Abundantly

———— ∮ ————

Dear Father,

I just came across Your words in John where You say You sent Your Son to us that we may have life and have it more abundantly. I think You are saying there is more to life than just living it. You want more for us than that. You want us to live it to the fullest – to have all the joy Your Son had in sharing His life with others. You want us to share our lives and what we learn about His life with others – and that will help us all to live "more abundantly."

Abundance is said to be "more than enough." That forms a beautiful picture. You have such great plans for us if only we will open ourselves to them and listen to You and follow Your guidance.

Help me, Father, to focus on You. Help me to have that inner tingling all through me because I have "more than enough" – I have You and Your wonderful promises for me. But don't let me be satisfied with just that, either. Lead me to step out in faith to let others know, by my example, that You are filling and refilling and <u>overflowing</u> my life abundantly with Your goodness.

I am come that they might have life,
and that they might have it more abundantly.
John 10:10 (KJV)

Prayer

VOLUMES HAVE BEEN written about the subject of prayer. Jesus spoke often about prayer and the Bible lists many examples of Jesus praying, both in public and in private. He taught us how to pray when he gave us the Lord's Prayer in Matthew Chapter 6. He tells us in Matthew 21 that whatever we ask in prayer, we will receive if we have faith.

We should also remember that Jesus prayed all the time, not just in time of crisis. Timothy said prayer will help to produce a quiet, tranquil life. When we rush around looking for peace outside ourselves and our relationship with God, we can be sure our prayer life is defective. Paul said we should pray in the spirit on all occasions and with all kinds of prayers and requests. In Ephesians, Paul also asked for prayers for himself so he could make known the mystery of the gospel to all who would listen. Later, Paul referred to our bodies as a Temple of God (I Cor. 6:19). When I think of a Temple I think of not only a holy place, but a quiet place. When I pray, I want to go "inside myself" to that quiet Temple. James challenges us to pray for one another and he added that the earnest prayer of a righteous man has great power and wonderful results.

It's been said that if our prayers had less of the tail feathers of pride and more wing, they would be all the better. If a plane carries all of its passengers or cargo in the tail, it will never get off the ground. It needs to spread things out for balance. The same holds true for a ship or a sailboat. If all the passengers are on one side of the ship or the sailboat, it will lean precariously. This is a good reminder that proper balance is always necessary, in our daily lives as well as in our prayer life.

When you pray, begin with God and center on Him. Praise him. Don't just ask and thank and plead and complain. We need prayer every day! It should be our key for the day and our lock for the night. Prayer will not only change circumstances, it can change us. We need prayer for comfort and for blessing. Pray out loud now and then – it helps you to think better. Above all, <u>be specific</u>! Remember, it isn't the actual words we pray but the condition of our hearts as we pray that brings us peace. Short prayers are often long enough. It is not the length of your prayer but the strength that is desirable. Never forget as you pray that what God says to <u>you </u>is a thousand times more important than what you say to <u>Him</u>. Pause now and then and really listen! Remember, too, that your prayer life may need more "knee-ology."

God answers prayers in three different ways. Yes, no, and wait a while. His time and timings are different from our time. Prayers are a little like eggs; they don't always hatch as soon as they are laid.

A writer once compared prayer to our schooling. There is a grade school of prayer when we talk to God. There is an advanced school of prayer, like high school, when we allow Him to talk to us. Then there is the college and graduate level of "togetherness" which requires no words. We move up these levels by constantly putting our life at one with Christ.

Someone once said prayer is like the old-fashioned water pump. When it was not used, it stopped working until it was primed. The more it was pumped – and the oftener – the smoother the flow of water. The more we pray, the easier and more natural it becomes. When we put it off, it can become more and more difficult to get back into the groove – into the good habit of praying.

Prayer is withdrawing to be renewed by God. It is a respite to renew ourselves. Remember, when weary – withdraw. Prayer is not just a "fold-your-hands" exercise but a constant and on-going conversation with our Father all day so we can remain alert for the devil's tricks and for opportunities to serve the Lord. Make prayer a regular "rest stop" and relax in His love, His forgiveness, His presence, and you will be renewed and strengthened in His footsteps.

Now here are some P's of prayer for you: Private, personal, praising, profound, persistent, penitent, purifying, powerful, peace-giving, perennial, petitioning, and purging. We must put aside all pretext, pretense, playing around, pretending pleasantness, and piousness. The results of prayer can be purification, permeating peace and new personal power.

Lastly, here are some S's of prayer for you too: short, silent, spiritual, stimulating, strong, spontaneous, significant, simple, seeking, sincere, supplicating, submissive, sensible, sacred, specific, searching, sensitive, strengthening, serious and satisfying.

So do not fear, for I am with you; do not be dismayed,
for I am your God. I will strengthen you and help you; I will uphold you
with my righteous right hand. For I am the Lord, your God,
who takes hold of your right hand and says to you,
do not fear; I will help you.
Isaiah 41:10-13

Artist

———— ◊ ————

As WE LIVE, our lives are like a canvas, and the life we live is painting a picture. The colors on our palette are decided and placed there by our wise Heavenly Father. Although we do not choose the colors, we must use what we are given. God guides the brush and He also controls the palette as He selects the colors to be used in our life's painting. The picture we present will depend on how we accept the mixing and the placement of our colors.

Our palettes may consist of darks, mediums and light shades – of quiet tones, pastels and also many more vivid, vibrant colors. Interestingly enough, the darker shades of grief, sorrow and disappointment are just as important – and as necessary – to the final effect as the bright, brilliant, happy colors. We must not fear or question these darker parts. Background shades may appear to be blotchy and dark – or be muted and even blurred, but sometimes these touches are needed to enrich the bright colors and to accent the lines of the main design that are to follow.

Many details of the painting may seem to be quite meaningless until the last touches of color are added. Our wise Helper is there to assist in mixing colors to get just the right effect to display our lives.

Pray about your personal painting as you go through life. Be thankful and grateful for all the contrasts of color – and for each stroke of His brush as your canvas takes on the effects He creates. Pray for acceptance of the hard, long strokes as well as the dabs and light touches here and there. Pray that at your final unveiling in the eternities of heaven you will NOT be disappointed

– or ashamed – of the results. Pray also for the times when the brush seems to go over and over an area to make it "just right" in His eyes. He has a very clear idea of what the finished product is to be. The final showing of your work will be in His presence in Heaven. Pray that you will exude pride and radiate happiness as others view your canvas and your life as truly the work of the Master.

She selects wool and flax and works with eager hands.
Proverbs 31:13

In her hand she holds the distaff and grasps
the spindle with her fingers.
Proverbs 31:9

Tears

WEEPING AND TEARS are referred to many times in the bible. Many different types of tears are written about in both the Old and New Testament. There are remorseful tears in Genesis when Esau cried upon hearing Jacob had stolen his birthright. David shed sorrowful tears in Psalm 6. The sinful woman washed the feet of Jesus with her tears in Luke 7. Paul shed tears of anguish in II Corinthians 2 and in Acts 20 he wrote of anguished tears as he served the Lord in humility.

In Psalm 56 David is struggling as he is attacked and he fears for his life as he cries to the Lord asking him to save his tears in a bottle and to record them in His scroll. The Living Bible says they are preserved and recorded in a book.

What a beautiful picture this paints! Isn't this a delightful demonstration of His love and His caring? To think that my tears are so important to him that he saves them! He records them to keep track of them! Some of my tears have been such foolish tears! Many were a complete waste of my time and my energy. But then again, many were important because they helped me express my hurt, my fears, my anger, my joy, or my disappointment and utter frustration with a situation. But, futile or useful, he scooped up each one lovingly and put it in my bottle. He recorded all of them in my book. He comforted me and soothed me and helped me to prepare for a joy in the morning – facing things anew with him at my side.

Each of us has a protective film on our eyeballs that is constantly washing over them to cleanse and protect them. Our eyes will tear automatically if dirt or other foreign matter tries to penetrate this delicate area. This is what Jesus can be to us if we allow Him to work in our lives. He is like an unseen film constantly washing over us, cleansing and protecting us from the sin that seeks entry into our lives.

"For his anger lasts only a moment, but his favor lasts a lifetime;
weeping may remain for a night, but rejoicing comes in the morning."
Psalm 30:5

He will wipe every tear from their eyes. There will be
no more death or mourning or crying or pain,
for the old order of things has passed assay.
Revelations 21:4

The Lord is my light and my salvation – whom shall I fear?
The Lord is the stronghold of my life – of whom shall I be afraid?
Psalm 27:1

New

---- § ----

As I WRITE this, we have just moved into a new year on our calendars. Many see this as a new start – a time for changing ourselves in some way – for beginning again, or beginning anew. It's a time to put aside our old ways and bad habits and strengthen our resolve to become better informed and more focused, and to use our time in a more meaningful fashion. But, in reality, when you get right down to it, a new year simply means changing the dates on our calendars. Granted, we can make promises or resolutions to improve ourselves, but, if we do, those changes come from the inside out and not because of a new number on our calendars.

There are many references to new things in the Bible. The Psalmist David often referred to a new song and to a new spirit and a new heart as a result. In Psalm 40 David says: *"He put a new song in my mouth, a hymn of praise to our God. Many will see and hear and put their trust in the Lord."* David is recalling his experiences of God's help in the past in his time of trouble. These experiences often moved him to praise and it moved others to faith.

Later, in Psalm 98:1 David says: *"Sing to the Lord a new song, for he has done marvelous things; his right hand and his holy arm have worked salvation for him."* This is the NIV version. The King James says *"O Sing unto the Lord a new song; for he hath done marvelous things; his right hand, and his holy arm, hath gotten him the victory."* In the Living Bible, the wording is just a bit different. It says: *"Sing a new song to the Lord telling about his mighty deeds! For he has won a mighty victory by his power and holiness."* This is a call to celebrate with joy. The first 3 stanzas of this Psalm progressively extend the call to ever widening circles – the congregation at the temple, all peoples of the earth, and then the whole of creation.

The entire 9 verses of Psalm 149 are filled with praise and joy in the Lord. It starts out by saying: *"Praise the Lord. Sing to the Lord a new song, his praise in the assembly of the saints."*

The prophet Ezekiel also refers to things being new in his book in the Old Testament. In Ezekiel 18:31 he says: *"Rid yourselves of all your offenses you have committed, and get a new heart and a new spirit."* This verse then goes on to say *"Repent and live."*

In the New Testament in Matthew Jesus is talking to his disciples and in Chapter 9 he says, *"No one sews a patch of unshrunk cloth on an old garment, for the patch will pull away from the garment, making the tear worse. Neither do men pour new wine into old wineskins. If they do, the skins will burst, the wine will run out and the wineskins will be ruined. No, they pour new wine into new wineskins, and both are preserved."* In ancient times, goatskins were used to hold wine. As the fresh grape juice fermented, the wine would expand, and the new wineskin would stretch with it. But a used skin that had already been stretched would break if new wine were poured into it. When we accept Jesus and make him a part of our lives, He brings a newness with Him that cannot be confined within the old forms. These same words are repeated again in Mark 2 and Luke 5.

In Galatians 6:14-15, Paul says this: *"May I never boast except in the cross of our Lord Jesus Christ, through which the world has been crucified to me, and I to the world. Neither circumcision nor uncircumcision means anything; what counts is a new creation."* Paul is saying than when we are in Christ, or when we become a child of God, we undergo a transformation that results in an entirely new being. It's like creation takes place again.

In 2 Peter 3:13, Peter says, *"But in keeping with his promise we are looking forward to a new heaven and a new earth, the home of righteousness."* Earlier in this chapter Peter tells us this: *"But the day of the Lord will come like a thief. The heavens will disappear with a roar; the elements will be destroyed by fire, and the earth and everything in it will be laid bare. Since everything will be destroyed in this way, what kind of people ought you to be? You ought to live holy and godly lives as you look forward to the day of God."*

I like the way the Living Bible expresses these two verses from I John. *"Dear brothers, I am not writing out a new rule for you to obey, for it is an old one you have always had, right from the start. You have heard it all before. Yet, it is always new, and works for you just as it did for Christ; and as we obey this commandment, to love one another, the darkness in our lives disappears and the new light of life in Christ shines."* Then the Living Bible goes on to say: *"The person who has been born into God's family does not make a practice of sinning, because now God's life is in him; so he can't keep on sinning, for this new life has been born into him and controls him – he has been born again."* In other words, he is a new creation.

Let's all strive to be a part of God's new creation by fulfilling His plan for us and for our lives. We don't have to wait for a calendar to tell us it's time for changes. If we listen, the Holy Spirit will tell us almost daily not only what we need to change and also how to go about it if we are willing. Isn't it wonderfully comforting to know we don't have to wait for a new year because we can start fresh anytime the spirit moves us to want to be closer to God? How lucky we are! His hand is already stretched out to receive and guide us!

Then he turned to his disciples and said privately,
"Blessed are the eyes that see what you see. For I tell you that
many prophets and kings wanted to see what you see but did not see it,
and to hear what you hear but did not hear it."
Luke 10:23, 24

Sharing

§

OH, LORD, REMIND me to share! Don't let me forget how important that little gesture can be! I don't mean money, Father. I mean myself – and you! Why, with Your help, I could probably even do both at the same time!

What an exciting thought, Lord! You gave us such a tremendous example by sharing Your beloved Son with us. You gave Him to be with us in earthly form for a while and now we can have Him with us all the time, wherever we are, through the Holy Spirit, as our Comforter, our Redeemer.

I feel so blessed to have that gift from You. Help me to share this gift! I want others to know You as I do. Help me to share You – and me. I want others to be just as excited as I am!

And we pray this in order that you
may live a life worthy of the Lord and may please him in every way;
bearing fruit in every good work, growing in the knowledge of God, being
strengthened with all power according to his glorious might
so that you may have great endurance and patience.
Colossians 1:10

Round

─────── § ───────

WE ARE SURROUNDED by round things in our lives – circles of one sort or another. The earth, the sun, the moon and all the planets are round. (I once read that if the sun were hollow, it could contain more than 100 million worlds the size of our earth!)

Jesus wore a round crown of thorns during His final hours of persecution and death. A short while later, the round stone was removed from the entrance to His tomb to signify His glorious resurrection.

Years ago a high stone wall and a moat went around a castle as a form of protection against any who might bring harm to those who lived inside the wall. If danger threatened, a drawbridge could be raised to prevent the enemy from entering the castle grounds or the town.

An engagement ring is round and then a wedding ring is round – and later a teething ring can be round. These rings help us form the circle of life.

Once we seal ourselves with the stamp of Christ we become part of the Circle of Christianity and that's one time I'm happy to be going around in circles!!

Following is a poem I wrote about my daughter at the time of her marriage:

Cynthia Irish Hockins

CIRCLES

A stone dropped in still water
Creates circles reaching out.
My first life circle was in the womb
As I was formed.
The next, my family circle
After I was born.

A teething ring, class ring, engagement ring, wedding ring
Each helped me grow outwardly
And then – back to the circle of the womb
As my child formed and grew.
My family circle now began anew.

My child's ring of life now leaves mine
To create her own ongoing circle of life;
And yet, mine is still intact!
I will not lose by sharing her.
My circle rests, and now I can rejoice as
I watch her circle grow.

Doctor

—— ∮ ——

WHEN WE THINK there is something wrong with us physically or emotionally, the best decision we can make is to see a doctor or professional person who specializes in the treatment of our particular complaints. This person will listen to our symptoms, make notes in our personal record, evaluate any possible solutions, and then recommend the best possible tests and medications to treat us, hopefully in terms we can understand.

When our spiritual lives go astray, we need to see the best doctor ever – our wise, all-knowing Lord and Heavenly Father. As we tell Him our deepest concerns and lay out all our problems, He listens quietly, evaluates the best solutions, lovingly forgives us for any wrongdoing and helps us stand up, tall and proud – and best of all, we stand forgiven! Now we're ready to start fresh. Aren't we lucky that He is extremely well trained in the school of forgiveness and fresh starts?!

The Lord is my rock, my fortress, and my deliverer;
My God is my rock, in whom I take refuge.
He is my shield and the horn of my salvation, my stronghold.
Psalm 18:1

Holy Spirit

THE HOLY SPIRIT has been around since the days of creation. On the day of Pentecost we learn that the Holy Spirit entered the bodies of the Disciples. The Bible describes it as a sound like the blowing of a violent wind coming from heaven and filling the whole house where they were sitting. Acts 2:4 says they were all filled with the Holy Spirit and they began to speak in other tongues as the Spirit enabled them. Jesus told them that all of His words had been given to Him by the power of the Holy Spirit.

This Holy Spirit can be likened to an electric current going through us. It can be turned on or off, but we must always be connected to the Power Source of God. In Romans we are told there is life through the Spirit. Paul says more about the Holy Spirit in this one chapter than we can find anywhere else in the Bible with the exception of Chapters 14-16 in the Book of John.

The Holy Spirit is the presence of God in our lives. It helps us in three different ways. It helps us <u>inwardly</u> by granting us the fruits of the Spirit as mentioned in Galatians 5:22-24; it helps us <u>upwardly</u> by praying for us as written in Romans 8:26; and it helps us <u>outwardly</u> by pouring God's love into our hearts as it says in Romans 5:5. We must be tuned into the spirit, receptive in our souls, and alert in our attitudes, in order to detect the impact of His presence upon our path.

Where the devil shows us all of our faults at one time to disarm and disable us, the Holy Spirit shows us one fault at a time and helps us deal with it. It gives us gifts to handle each new opportunity as well as each challenge we face. We cannot store up these gifts and save them as we would an endowment. These gifts are given for a particular reason and for a specific purpose and at a specific time. We do not move ahead by knowing all that lies ahead of us. We move ahead because the Holy Spirit is with us. It is in us, urging us forward and, thankfully, walking with us.

Jesus came to the disciples on that Day of Pentecost with a greeting and with a blessing of peace, and then He gave them the gift of the Holy Spirit. Let's go forward into the world embracing this same peaceful blessing and this glorious God-given gift.

In the same way, the Spirit helps us in our weakness.
We do not know what we ought to pray, but the Spirit himself
intercedes for us with groans that words cannot express.
And he who searches our hearts knows the mind of the Spirit,
because the Spirit intercedes for the saints in accordance with God's will.
Romans 8:26

And hope does not disappoint us,
because God has poured out his love into our hearts
by the Holy Spirit, whom he has given us.
Romans 5:5

Fruits of the Spirit

———— § ————

In the Bible, the book of Galatians was written by Paul to the people of Galatia when he visited them on his second journey. Paul opens this book with grace and peace to the people of Galatia in Chapter 1 and he closes with grace as a blessing at the end of Chapter 6. Galatians is often called "Luther's Book" because Martin Luther quoted Paul as he wrote and argued against the theology he was opposing at the beginning of The Reformation. Paul – and Martin Luther – stressed that it is by grace through faith that a man (or a woman) is justified, and it is by faith alone that he is to live out his new life in the freedom of the Spirit.

Paul lists the Fruits of the Spirit in Galatians 5:22 when he says, *"But the fruit of the spirit is love, joy, peace, patience, kindness, goodness, faithfulness, gentleness and self-control."* He is saying that if we live by the spirit we are, in effect, carrying each other's burdens. If we have love in our hearts, the other fruits are almost sure to follow. By living with joy we will experience a peace that only God can give and we will become more patient and kind. If we are patient and kind, goodness and faithfulness will be more natural to us, and we will experience gentleness and all of these things lead to a form of self-control. We are controlling our emotions and choosing to live by the fruits of the spirit and for the results that such living can bring to our hearts and our lives – and to the lives of those around us as well.

Paul reminds us in Chapter 6 that we will reap what we sow. If we sow to please a sinful nature, we will reap destruction – but if we sow to please the Spirit – or to please God – we will reap the reward of eternal life. He goes on to say that as opportunities present themselves, we should strive to do good to all people.

In the book of Ephesians, also written by Paul, he reminds us that before we came to be identified as children of God we lived in a form of darkness. By becoming believers and children of God we entered the Light. In Ephesians 5:9 he said that the fruit of the light consists in all goodness, righteousness and truth, and he reminds us that light is productive because it encourages growth. James 5:7 reminds us to be patient until the Lord's coming. As an example he points to the farmer waiting patiently for the land to yield its valuable crop following the warmth and rains of summer. James encourages us to persevere.

The fruits of the spirit – all nine of them – each pose a challenge to us, but the end result is truly a reward worth pursuing. Living in love will instill a joy and a peace. Patience will encourage kindness, goodness and faithfulness. Gentleness and self-control encourage love – and joy – and we find ourselves part of a beautiful, endless circle with God at the center.

Since we live by the Spirit, let us keep in step with the Spirit.
Let us not become conceited, provoking and envying each other.
Galatians 5:25-26

Mail

THE MAIL JUST came with a letter from my sister! Thank you, Lord! Thank You that she thought of me and took the time to tell me so. Thank You for the little mundane things that fill her pages because they tell me about her life. They tell me how she fills her time and how she feels. Not only how she feels about others, but that she cares enough about me to share even the smallest details of her life.

Thank You that I have a sister, Lord. She means the world to me! We have shared more than parents and home and a brother – we have shared each other and we have shared You!

She has such a gracious, loving way about her – and yet she, too, is human. Be with her when she needs You – watch over her and be with her always. I miss her and often feel frustrated by these miles that separate us. Help me when I write to her to be as sharing and as caring of my time and my thoughts. Let her feel my love flowing to her as hers does to me.

Like cold water to a weary soul is good news
from a distant land. Proverbs 25:25

A Joy in Jesus

There's a joy in knowing Jesus and in learning how He bore

all my sins and then died for me and came back to life once more.

There's a joy in pleasing Jesus for that pleases others too.

And the Christian life He offers can also belong to you!

Share my joy and come to know Him! You'll feel better than before!

Happy times await you, Christian! No one else can offer more!

Talents

THE DICTIONARY DEFINES the word talent as "the abilities, powers and gifts bestowed upon a person; natural endowments; thought of as a divine trust; a natural capacity or gift." My Bible Concordance also describes it as a unit of weight with one talent weighing approximately 75 pounds. In monetary language, a talent was worth more than a thousand dollars.

In Ephesians 4:11 Paul wrote: *"Some of us have been given special ability as apostles; to others he has given the gift of being able to preach well; some have special ability in winning people to Christ, helping them to trust Him as their Savior; still others have a gift for caring for God's people as a shepherd does his sheep, leading and teaching them in the ways of God."*

In Matthew Chapter 25 Jesus teaches the disciples through a series of Parables. One of these parables dealt with a landowner who was going on a journey and he asked 3 different men to care for his property in his absence. He also gave different monetary talents to each of these men, and when he returned from his travels he asked each to account for his handling of the talents entrusted to him. The first 2 explained how their talents had been increased because of their wise thinking. When the 3rd man was asked what he had done he said he had buried it so it would not be lost. The owner was bitter and angry and after scolding him, he cast him into the darkness and he proceeded to celebrate with the other two. Jesus was saying that our talents must be used in order that they may grow and be appreciated. If you bury or hide your individual talent, whatever it may be, you are depriving others as well as yourself.

If we think a talent is only singing, playing the piano, or the ability to entertain, etc., we are robbing others of God's many kinds of blessings referred to in I Peter, chapter 4 where Peter says, *"God has given each of you some special abilities; be sure to use them to help each other, passing on to others God's many kinds of blessings."* Unless we use the talents God gives us, they will not multiply. Talents or endowments are not necessarily distributed equally, and with the gift of any talent there is also a responsibility. The talent is only the beginning! What we do with it and how we share it is the other part of the gift! One talent (or challenge) we are ALL given is to make our Lord Jesus known to others.

Here are examples of other things I believe should be considered talents:

...Listening when someone else is speaking.
...Speaking with loving tact, whether to a family member or a stranger.
...Being on time.
...Following through with commitments.
...Being cheerful, even when you don't feel like it.
...Being hospitable, both at home and at church.

Hospitality is not only a talent, it is truly a gift. Our lives are enriched when we practice it. Hospitality should focus on serving, not on impressing. In Genesis, Abraham offered food and rest to three strangers, and by doing this, he hosted angels unawares. In Romans 12:13 Paul says, *"Contribute to the needs of the saints; practice hospitality."* Someone once said that the best indicator of our Christian love is the way we welcome strangers. Jesus did so, usually with open arms – and He was often criticized for His association with sinners.

Let's each ask God to show us where our own personal talents lie. Ask Him to show us which ones need to be improved upon so we may maximize our talents and begin sharing them. By doing this, these talents will become a more natural part of our everyday life. They will become a habit – and <u>some</u> habits can be good ones!

> *"Each one should use whatever gift he has received*
> *to serve others, faithfully administering God's grace in its various forms.*
> *If anyone speaks, he should do it as one speaking*
> *the very words of God.*
> *If anyone serves, he should do it with the strength God provides,*
> *so that in all things God may be praised through Jesus Christ.*
> *To him be the glory and the power for ever and ever. Amen."*
> *I Peter 4:10, 11*

The Knots Prayer

(Author Unknown - but Known to God)

Dear God:
Please untie the knots
that are in my mind, my heart and my life.
Remove the have nots, the can nots and the do nots
that I have in my mind.

Erase the will nots,
may nots, might nots that may find
a home in my heart

Release me from the could nots,
would nots and should nots that obstruct my life.

And most of all, Dear God,
I ask that you remove from my mind, my heart and my life
all of the 'am nots' that I have allowed to hold me back,
especially the thought that I am not good enough.
Amen.

Shadows

I THOUGHT ABOUT shadows today, Lord, as I watched one creep across the patio, inching its way toward the back fence. It moved slowly across me and then it covered me.

I can be in the shadow of something else – or I can cast my own shadow. Sometimes it is little and all pushed together – and other times it is long and tall and it spreads way out. Either way, it suggests something nearby.

A shadow is always moving, isn't it? It can be a shelter or a protective cover. It can also be a reflected image – or an inseparable companion. David refers to our life span as a shadow in I Chronicles 29:15 where he says, "For we are aliens and pilgrims before You, as were all our fathers; our days on earth are as a shadow and without hope."

After thinking it over, I've decided I want to be in your shadow, dear Father. I want your protective shadow all around me, sheltering me. Yet I also want to be a reflected image of You, which means I must cast my OWN shadow. Help me to be a shadow to someone else today, Lord – help me be their protection, their shelter. Help my shadow to grow and expand – and yet, don't let my shadow get too far from Yours at any time. Don't let my shadow attempt to overshadow Yours. When I turn around and face away from my shadow, let me always know Yours is there for me!

Abundant Sonshine

He who dwells in the shelter of the Most High
will rest in the shadow of the Almighty. I will say to the Lord
"He is my refuge and fortress, my God, in whom I trust."
Psalm 91:1-2

Comfort

THE DICTIONARY SAYS the word comfort means to offer relief to someone in distress – someone who may be in physical pain due to an illness or disease, or in emotional pain due to a death or a loss of some kind. It also says comforting is a means of soothing, of encouraging, aiding or helping someone. This act implies a giving because you are helping or comforting someone else. In this way you can offer comfort and you can also be a comfort.

A family was having a conversation at the dinner table one night about which verse in the Bible was their favorite and why. When they came to the youngest child she said that her favorite Bible verse was the one about the quilt. When they questioned her about this, she said Jesus told His disciples He was going to go away but He was sending them a comforter so they wouldn't feel alone and they could wrap themselves in this comforter. What a beautiful way to think of the word comfort because through this "quilt" that He offers, we are "covered" with Christ's robe of righteousness. We are comforted with His promises.

There is an old saying puts it very well. It says: God comforts us not so we will be comfortable, but so that we will be comforters. He came to comfort – to reassure – and He recognizes we often need comfort, but he also wants us to be a comfort to others from our own experiences.

In John 14 He comforts His disciples with these words: *"Do not let your hearts be troubled. Trust in God; trust also in me. In my Father's house are many rooms; if it were not so, I would have told you. I am going there to prepare a place for you. And if I go and prepare a place for you, I will come back and take you to be with me that you also may be where I am."*

When Jesus was dying on the cross, even in the midst of His excruciating pain, he gave comfort to others. He saw his mother standing next to John, the disciple whom he loved, and he said to Mary, *"Dear woman, here is your son."* Then he turned to John and said, *"Here is your mother."* The Bible goes on to say that from that time on, the disciple took her into his home. Jesus offered them both comfort in their time of grief, and he gave each of them the opportunity to BE a comfort to the other.

Later in that same chapter he says: *"If you love me, you will obey what I command. And I will ask the Father, and he will give you another counselor to be with you forever – the Spirit of truth."* That is our promise of the Holy Spirit as a part of our lives. We each have our own personal Counselor, our own personal Comforter. Let's go forward today, wrapped in the Spirit of the Lord, and let's be both comforted and comforting.

> *Praise be to the God and Father of our Lord Jesus Christ, the Father of compassion and the God of all comfort, who comforts us in all our troubles, so that we can comfort those in any trouble with the comfort we ourselves have received from God.*
> *II Corinthians 1:3,4*

Baker

———— § ————

HAVE YOU EVER thought of God as a Master Baker? First, He gathered all the necessary ingredients that make up my life. He carefully measured them and then gently mixed and folded them all together. Then He added Himself to the batter of my life in the form of yeast so He could help me expand and grow. He then covered me in the warmth of His loving arms, under his protective wings, so this yeast could "work" and I could "rise."

He is truly the leaven in my life and He is also what keeps me from falling apart sometimes. This yeast reaches into every corner of my being. It is totally invisible so no one can see that it is there, but if it is reacting as yeast should, God will radiate out through me and others will recognize that He is an important part of my life! Once He is thoroughly "mixed" into my being, no one can ever take Him away! He is part of my life from that moment on! Isn't that amazing?

Here are some interesting facts about yeast:

(1) It shows extensive internal power
(2) It is invisible to the eye
(3) It is absorbed in what it surrounds.
(4) Once added, it cannot be taken away
(5) It suggests a silent working
(6) In the Old Testament it was a symbolic renouncement of sin, and a rededication to the Lord.

Pray that God will work in us and through us as He mixes the ingredients of our lives, and that He will surround us and hold us together, especially when we need Him the most.

> *"The kingdom of heaven is like yeast that a woman took and mixed into a large amount of flour until it worked all through the dough."*
> *Matthew 13:13 - The Parable of the Yeast*

Psalm 139

A FEW VERSES from this Psalm were read recently as a part of the Sunday morning lesson at our church service. I've read this Psalm several times before, but hearing the verses read aloud really jolted my thinking processes and after the service that day I went home and read the entire Psalm out loud to myself. Again, I was just amazed at my reactions to these words. This Psalm says it all! It says God knows us inside and out -- He knows our every thought and deed, our every action and reaction, because He knew us even before we were born and He had already laid out a life plan for us as individuals. He knew every hair on my head and how tall I'd be and what size shoe I would wear before I was born! I particularly liked verse 5 where it says *You hem me in -- behind and before; you have laid your hand upon me.* The study notes in my NIV Bible explain these phrases beautifully. #1, to hem me in is *"to keep me under scrutiny."* Scrutiny means a close examination, continuous watch, or a lengthy searching look. Doesn't that make you feel important? Don't you feel special that God cares that much about every little detail of your life? I really like the "behind and before" part too. Before I do something he knows about it - and after it's done, regardless of the consequences, he knows that too. Good, bad or otherwise, he helps me deal with it! The 2nd part of that verse says *"you have laid your hand upon me."* The study notes for this verse say he is keeping constant individual watch so we cannot escape his scrutiny. Job 13:27 says something similar when Job says God is keeping close watch on all my paths by putting marks on the soles of my feet. In ancient Babylonia there was a practice of putting a mark on the soles of the feet of slaves to identify who they belonged to so they couldn't escape. God "marks us" as His own by placing his hands on us as we go about our daily lives. That's a beautiful thought -- truly a loving gesture from a loving God.

The Psalm goes on to say there is no hiding from God. Not even darkness can hide us from God's sight. His hand is there guiding us, comforting us -- no matter what our needs are and no matter what we do, He is there as our loving caretaker. David then reminds himself that God knit him together in his mother's womb and he praises God because he was fearfully and wonderfully made.

Later in verse 23 he says *"Search me, O God, and know my heart....and lead me in the way everlasting."* He's asking God to examine him, to help him maintain his integrity and to maintain his devotion so he can continue to be true to God. At this point, my Bible notes make reference to Psalm 16 verses 9-11: *Therefore my heart is glad and my tongue rejoices; my body also will rest secure because you will not abandon me to the grave, nor will you let your Holy One see decay. You have made known to me the path of life; you will fill me with joy in your presence, with eternal pleasures at your right hand."*

I challenge you to read through this Psalm occasionally. Make it a part of your personal devotions often because it is a special reminder of how important God thinks we each are and how mindful He is of our every thought, deed and action. Rejoice in knowing you are indeed fearfully and wonderfully made!

> *Though I walk in the midst of trouble, you pre-*
> *serve my life; you stretch out your hand against*
> *the anger of my foes, with your right hand you save*
> *me. The Lord will fulfill his purpose*
> *for me; your love, O Lord, endures forever.*
> *Psalm 138:7-8*

Seven

—— § ——

SOME PEOPLE THINK of the number seven as a "lucky number." Personally, I believe we make our own "luck." I don't believe things happen by chance, be they good or bad. Maybe that "lucky" designation came about because of the numerous times this number appears in the Bible.

Genesis, the first book of the Bible, begins by telling about the creation. In the beginning, God created seven categories. These are: earth, light, firmament, dry land and vegetation, moon and stars, birds and fish, animals and man. The Bible tells us he did all of this in six days and on the seventh day he rested. Later, in Exodus 23, we are told to work six days and to rest on the seventh, thus completing a cycle. In that same chapter, when the people were receiving the laws of God through Moses, they were told to work the land for six years and let it lie fallow the seventh year.

In Genesis 6 God was disappointed with mankind and He gave instructions to Noah to build a huge ark to protect him, his family and pairs of animals. In Genesis 7 he told Noah to take his family and the animals into the ark and they were in the ark seven days before the rains came to flood the earth. In Genesis 9, when the rains stopped and the waters receded, God promised Noah this flooding would never happen again and He made a covenant with Noah and all of his descendants in the form of a rainbow. This rainbow consisted of seven colors, as do all the rainbows we see yet today. The seven colors are red, orange, yellow, green, blue, indigo and violet. A rainbow is a beautiful, rare occurrence, and each color reminds us of God's wonderful promises and His deep and abiding love and care for each of us. (By the way, I understand a rainbow is actually a whole circle but we only see part of it because the earth gets in the way. Also, we only see the rainbow if the sun is behind us to reflect it.) When Jacob returned to his country with all of his family and his flocks, he bowed to Esau seven times in an attitude of asking for forgiveness and reconciliation. He <u>was</u> forgiven, and they <u>were</u> reconciled.

In Exodus Moses spoke of seven plagues while he dealt with Pharaoh on behalf of his people. The seven plagues were frogs, lice, flies, animals, boils, hail, and locusts. In Leviticus, Moses saw to the building of the first Tabernacle after receiving detailed, explicit instructions from God. When it was completed and ready for use, Moses anointed the altar seven times to consecrate it as God had directed. In addition to the altar, he consecrated all the utensils and the basin with its stand, seven times. Then, at God's command, Moses told Aaron and his sons to stay at the entrance to the Tent of Meeting for seven days to complete their ordination.

In I Kings Ahab told Elijah to look for a cloud as he prayed for rain and he told him to go look again and again, a total of seven times. He did this, and the rains came. In Judges Samson's hair was braided in seven locks. In 2 Chronicles Solomon took seven years to build a temple for the Lord and a palace for himself. Proverbs speaks of the seven things the Lord hates. They are haughtiness, lying, murder, plotting evil, eagerness to do wrong, a false witness and sowing discord among brothers.

The book of Isaiah also makes a couple references to the number seven. It says seven women will argue for one man after God's judgment falls on them. God said there would be so few men left that seven women will fight over one man begging that all seven be allowed to marry him. Later, Isaiah says the Lord will dry a path through the Red Sea and divide it into seven streams that can be crossed.

In the New Testament, the number appears again many times. In Matthew, when Jesus was ready to feed the 4000, he began with seven loaves of bread and finished with seven baskets of leftover pieces. In the book of John, Christ performed seven miracles before His death. Matthew also makes reference to Peter asking how often he should forgive someone and Jesus answered him by saying, *"I tell you, not seven times, but seventy-seven times."*

Jesus said seven words or phrases as He hung on the cross. Luke 23:34 says *(1) "Father, forgive them for they know not what they do,"* and in v. 43 He is speaking to the thief next to him when he says, *(2) "Truly I say to you, today you will be with me in Paradise."* Next, in John 19:26 He speaks to His mother Mary and says, *(3) "Woman, behold thy son."* Both Matthew 27:46 and Mark 15:34 tell us he said *(4) "My God, My God, why have you forsaken me?"* As the agony progressed, in John 19:28 he uttered *(5)" I thirst,"* and in verse 30 he said *(6) "It is finished."* His very last words are given in Luke 23:46 when he said, *(7) "Father, into thy hands I commit my spirit."* Notice that His first and last words were to His Heavenly Father.

II Peter lists the seven virtues. These are faith, knowledge, temperance, patience, godliness, brotherly kindness, and charity. In the Book of Revelations John addresses the seven churches in Asia. He also makes reference to the seven golden lamp stands, the seven stars the Lord holds in his hands, and to seven angels, each holding a trumpet.

Perhaps we should think of the number seven as being a complete number rather than a lucky one. Our luck is really that we are each a child of God and a member of His family, now and forever, in this world and in eternity.

Abundant Sonshine

And we know that in all things God works for the good
of those who love him, who have been called according to his purpose.
Romans 8:28

What, then, shall we say in response to this?
If God is for us, who can be against us?
He who did not spare his own Son, but gave him up for us all —
how will he not also, along with him, graciously give us all things?
Romans 8:31-33

Laundry Day

LORD, TODAY IS laundry day. It is a chore, but I want you to know I really do not mind it! I smiled when I came across the nightgown turned inside-out. She wore it to bed that way the other night and when I commented on it, she said, "It's okay, Mom – tomorrow night it'll be right-side-in after I pull it over my head in the morning!" Such logic, Lord! Why didn't I think of that? I'm SO lucky she's mine!

Next I smiled at my boy's jeans with the tiny tear in the knee. He'd had such a good time roughhousing outdoors with the guys that day and he was afraid I'd be angry – but even little tears in jeans are part of growing, aren't they? He's so full of love, and I'm so lucky he's mine!

And then I came to the socks all rolled in a ball – and that could only be you-know-who! I should feel lucky! Not every husband does that for his wife!

Thank you for these clothes to wash and bless the people who wear them. Keep them safe today please! Thanks, too, for the smudges on the towels and those who put them there. Thanks for helping me think good thoughts as I go about these routine things in my life. It's nice to feel needed! It takes the real "work" out of it and replaces it with "love!"

Abundant Sonshine

She sets about her work vigorously; her arms
are strong for her tasks.
Proverbs 31:17

She watches over the affairs of her household
and does not eat the bread of idleness.
Proverbs 31:27

Requirements

—§—

ONE OF THE dictionary definitions of the word requirement is this: A requirement is a necessity – it is something needed or even demanded. According to my Bible concordance although it is often a request, it can also be a necessary demand.

We are told in the Bible in Exodus that God spoke to Moses on the mountain and gave him instructions to be repeated to his people. Moses relayed these words to the people in Deuteronomy 10:12 where he says, *"And now, O Israel, what does the Lord your God ask of you (or require of you) but to fear the Lord your God, to walk in all his ways, to love him, to serve the Lord your God with all your heart and with all your soul, and to observe the Lord's commands and decrees that I am giving you for your own good."*

In Joshua 22:5 Joshua quotes Moses and repeats these same words. He says we are to *"Love the Lord your God, to walk in all his ways, to obey his commands, to hold fast to him and to serve him with all your heart and all your soul."* In Deuteronomy 11 God challenges the people to *"Fix these words of mine in your hearts and minds; tie them as symbols on your hands and bind them on your foreheads."* He encourages them to *"Teach them to your children, talking about them when you sit at home and when you walk along the road, when you lie down and when you get up."* He could have just said "do it all the time," but please note that He was far more specific. He left nothing to chance or to misinterpretation.

Later, in Micah 6:8 the prophet Micah says: *"And what does the Lord require of you? To act justly and love mercy and to walk humbly with your God."* When you break this verse down, we are being told to live our own lives and not interfere in the lives of others; we are to exhibit compassion in our dealings with others whether they are Christian or non-Christian; and we are to refrain from harming or punishing others. In other words, we are to mind our own business. We are told we should live in a forgiving and merciful manner. Mercy can also be described as *"kindness in excess of what may be expected."* We are also to walk humbly with our God. Humility is unpretentious – it is also modest and not self-centered.

We have certain physical requirements that enable us to exist. We require food and water for our physical well-being – and personally, I think we should add the requirement of a personal relationship with our Lord Jesus Christ. We should also write these words on our hearts and etch them into our minds.

*"When you make a vow to God, do not delay in fulfilling it. He has
no pleasure in fools; fulfill your vow. It is better not to vow
than to make a vow and not fulfill it.
Ecclesiastes 5:4, 5*

Geologist - Sculptor

ALTHOUGH THE WORDS "geologist" and "sculptor" are not mentioned in the Bible, I believe both of these terms are descriptive of God and our Lord Jesus Christ. The dictionary definition of geology says it is the science of dealing with the physical nature of the earth and the development of its crust and interior. It also refers to rocks, fossil forms, etc. As a geologist, and somewhat of a scientist, God established the nature of the earth and saw to its formation and development, inside and outside.

The dictionary definition of the word sculpture says it is the art of shaping stone, clay, wood, etc., into statues, figures, etc., or into another form. It can also mean to cut, carve, or chisel – to create or to design. God certainly did that, too, when he created Adam out of the dust of the earth and then He created Eve from one of Adam's ribs. God also created each of us in our mother's wombs, and magically and thankfully, he formed each of us in his own image. He is indeed our "Living Stone."

Jesus, because of his strength and magnitude, has often been referred to as the Rock of Ages – and our one true foundation. He is indeed our Rock and our foundation! He is our Living Stone and the Cornerstone on which we build our lives!

We are so very blessed that God is such a thoughtful, loving and caring God. He tends to each and every detail of our lives, inside and out. When we pray we should remember to thank Him for creating us and also for creating this beautiful world in which we live.

Abundant Sonshine

*As you come to him, the living Stone – rejected by men but
chosen by God and precious to him – you, also, like living stones,
are being built into a spiritual house to be a
holy priesthood, offering spiritual sacrifices acceptable to
God through Jesus Christ.*
I Peter 2:4-5

The American Eagle

THE AMERICAN EAGLE is a very interesting bird. It builds the largest nest of any North American bird or animal and it also builds the largest tree nest. These nests can be more than 5 feet tall and exceed 5 feet in diameter - and they can weigh up to one ton. There was one found in Ohio that was 8 1/2 feet across and 12 feet tall! The male and female are identical in plumage but the female is about 25% larger. At maturity the body length will be between 28 to 40" and the wingspan can be from 5.9 feet to 7.5 feet. Their size varies by their location and distance from the Equator. The smallest are in Florida and the largest are in Alaska where the female can weigh up to 17 pounds and have an 8 foot wingspan. They can fly at speeds of about 35+ miles per hour when gliding and flapping, and at about 30 miles per hour when they are carrying fish. Their dive speed can be up to 100 miles per hour although they seldom dive vertically. They can carry 4-8 pounds of food in their grasp. The beak and feet of the eagle are bright yellow-orange. The legs are feather-free, and the toes are short and powerful with large talons. The highly developed talon of the hind toe is used to pierce the vital areas of prey while it is held immobile by the front toes. The beak is large and hooked.

The dictionary gives a good description of the eagle. It is described as a very large and strong bird with sharp vision and powerful wings. I read elsewhere that eagles can see things that are up to 1 1/2 miles away. One who is eagle-eyed is said to have keen vision. The dictionary goes on to remind us that the eagle is the national symbol of the United States. Instead of seeking shelter when it rains, the eagle is the only bird that avoids rain by flying above the clouds. It is no wonder there are many Scriptural references to the eagle and it is no wonder God challenges us to "spread our wings" and "soar with eagles." What beautiful symbolism this brings to mind!

In 2 Samuel 1:23, Saul and Jonathan were described as being swifter than eagles and stronger than lions. Isaiah 40:31 is probably the best known Biblical reference to eagles. It says this: *"...but those who hope in the Lord will renew their strength. They will soar on wings like eagles; they will run and not grow weary; they will walk and not be faint."*

As the dictionary said, the Bald Eagle is the National Bird of the United States. On June 20, 1782, even before we had a United States President, the Continental Congress adopted the current design for the Great Seal of the U.S. which includes a Bald Eagle grasping 13 arrows and a 13-leaf olive branch with its talons. (George Washington took office in 1789.) The Bald Eagle appears on most official seals of the U.S. government, including the Seal of the U.S. President and the Presidential flag. The eagle has the longest life span among birds. About half-way through its life the eagle must make a difficult decision. Its long and flexible talons can no longer grab prey which serves as food. Its sharp beak becomes bent and its old and aged wings become heavy due to their thick feathers. These feathers stick to its chest making it difficult to fly. At that time, the eagle is left with only two options: it can die or it can go through a painful process of change which takes about 5-6 months.

I read that this process requires that the eagle fly to a mountain top and sit on its nest. There the eagle knocks its beak against a rock until it can pluck it out. After plucking it out, the eagle will wait for a new beak to grow and then it will pluck out its talons. When the new talons grow back, the eagle starts plucking out its old and aged feathers. After 5-6 months, with the new beak, new talons and new feathers, the eagle is ready to take a "flight of rebirth" and it often lives for many more years.

Often times, in order to survive, *we* have to begin a "change process" of our own. This often means spending time turning our thoughts inward so we can get rid of bad memories, old habits and other past traditions. Only when we stop constantly carrying our past burdens around can we take advantage of the present and spread our wings and soar with the eagles in our own personal "flight of rebirth." Why not write these words from Isaiah on a small piece of paper or a 3x5 card and put it on your bathroom mirror – or prop it on your kitchen windowsill – so you will see it often. Let this verse be a lovely reminder of God's love and of all He makes available to us as His children!

He gives strength to the weary and He increases the power of the weak.
Even youths grow tired and weary, and young men stumble and fall;
but those who hope in the Lord will renew their strength.
They will soar on wings like eagles;
they will run and not grow weary, they will walk and not be faint.
Isaiah 40:29-31

Courage

THE DICTIONARY DEFINES courage as a willingness to face and deal with danger, trouble or pain. It can also be described as fearlessness, and the dictionary also mentions bravery and valor as proper definitions. My Bible Concordance says it is fearlessness in the face of danger. There are many references to all kinds of courage all through the Bible, but I've selected a few I thought were interesting.

After the death of Moses God spoke to Joshua, son of Nun, who had been an aide to Moses. God charged him to prepare himself to lead the people who had been with Moses to cross the Jordan River to land that would then belong to the Israelites. God had made this promise to Moses. He said their territory would extend from the desert to Lebanon and from the Great River Euphrates to the Great Sea on the west. In Joshua 1:5 God says, *"No one will be able to stand up against you all the days of your life. I will never leave you or forsake you,"* and he goes on in verse 6 urging Joshua to be strong and courageous.

In Judges 7, God encouraged Gideon to attack an enemy camp and he provided him with encouraging intelligence information for this battle. A bit later, in I Samuel 4, the Lord told the Philistines to be strong and courageous and to "fight like men." They did fight and the Israelites were defeated during a great slaughter when Israel lost 30,000 foot soldiers and the Ark of the Covenant was captured.

In I Chronicles 28, David told his son, Solomon, to be strong and courageous as he saw to the building of The Temple. In verse 20 he says this: *"Be strong and courageous and do the work. Do not be afraid or discouraged for the Lord God, my God, is with you. He will not fail you or forsake you until all the work for the service of the temple of the Lord is finished."* David also admonished Solomon to acknowledge God and serve him with wholehearted devotion and a willing mind. He went on to say that the Lord searches every heart and understands every motive behind the thoughts.

Daniel was known as a visionary in his day. It is interesting to note that all of Daniel's visions showed God as being triumphant in the end. David lived in a time of great upheaval, not only in his home nation of Judah, but also the northern kingdom of Israel. Though he faced challenges, Daniel lived out his faith in time of distress. His life is a great example of how we can find hope in whatever circumstances we face. Each of us is called to be a Daniel – to be an example for the current generation. We have the choice of being poured into a mold, or – like Daniel – we can use this opportunity to become strengthened, to be bold, and to reflect the light of God in our lives.

Later, in Acts 27 in the New Testament, Paul urged his fellow travelers to keep up their courage as they tried to sail their way through terrible storms on their journey to Rome. He told them an angel of the Lord assured him that none of their lives would be lost although the ship would be destroyed.

In each of these examples, the Lord issued reassurances and encouragement against their fears. He kept them from becoming disheartened, afraid or discouraged. Fortunately, all of these events and many, many more are recorded in our Bibles so we can continue to be encouraged and uplifted when we need a fresh dose of courage. God was there then and God is here now.

Be on your guard; stand firm in the faith; be men of
courage; be strong. Do everything in love.
I Corinthians 16:13

Comparison of Jesus and Joseph

THERE ARE MANY interesting contrasts between the life of Joseph, the son of Jacob in the book of Genesis in the Old Testament and the life of Jesus throughout the New Testament. These contrasts include the following:

1. Joseph grew up with many brothers but he was not liked by them and he spent much time alone.
   Jesus was a "loner," always thinking ahead to what was expected of Him.
2. Joseph's father was an excellent witness with his faith and trust in the Lord.
   Jesus trusted His Father with His future and later with His life.
3. Both Joseph and Jesus were patient, willing, obedient, earnest and faithful.
4. Both were doubted, one by his brothers and the other by His disciples. They were each wrongfully accused and physically abused.
5. Neither complained and neither compromised.
6. Both were sold for a small amount of "blood money." Joseph was sold by his brothers for 20 shekels of silver, the price of a slave. Jesus was betrayed by Judas for 30 pieces of silver.

Thanksgiving

————— ◊ —————

THE CALENDAR SAYS it is November. There's a holiday coming up this later this month called Thanksgiving Day. I'm sure you've heard of it – it's the start of a long holiday weekend late in November. It comes just before the beginning of Advent in the Church year – and just a few weeks after the madness and monsters of Halloween. We don't hear nearly as much about Thanksgiving Day as we used to because once fall weather sets in we are bombarded in the stores and on the media with talks about Halloween and the accompanying costumes and pumpkins. There are even Halloween stores that specialize in unusual costumes and ornate decorations. And don't forget about the pumpkins! Some get carved or painted & trimmed – and some get eaten, but there's always an abundant supply everywhere we look. Houses and neighborhoods get decorated and kids are consumed with ideas about what costumes to wear and where they can go trick or treating for free candy. Even while we're having all that thrown at us from all directions, we are also being reminded that it's almost Christmas! There are Christmas stores open all year long in many areas and others open up just for the season. They offer a huge variety of elegant, fancy, whimsical tree effects and yard displays meant to entertain the masses. In addition to that we now have area merchants in shopping centers and malls devoting large sections of their stores to trees and ornaments and the toy manufacturers are well into their big holiday promotions. In the commercial world, Christmas means it is time for house and tree decorations and shopping for presents for friends and family and, of course, putting up the traditional decorated trees in our homes – and wreaths in our windows and yard lights too.

Somewhere in the midst of all this we come to Thanksgiving Day. Oh, there will be some talk of turkeys and the sharing of recipes for the best way to bake them. In recent years there has also much talk about how to boil them in large oil-filled outdoor cookers – and there is talk of parades to watch and pies to bake and the inevitable football games. But where is the <u>thanks</u> for it all. What has happened to talking about <u>why</u> we celebrate and bake and eat ourselves into a frenzy? When was the last time you heard a talk show host or a television newscaster say, "Today let's talk about the history of Thanksgiving and then we will talk about how thankful we all are for our many blessings."

When the day arrives many of us will sit down at a beautifully appointed table laid with fine china and silver and even cloth napkins! At some tables all will hold hands or they will fold hands in their laps, and someone usually says a nice prayer about thanks for the food and for the gathering – and then, not long after that, you push away from the table and the whole meaning of it all is forgotten! Sound familiar to you? Let's think about that for a minute!

There's something wrong here. Again I ask – where is the <u>thanks </u>in Thanksgiving? Why don't we hear more about the <u>why</u> of Thanksgiving? Our forefathers left lives of religious and personal persecution to sail across the ocean to a new land where they could then be free to serve their God and their families in ways they found acceptable – in ways that would never bring on severe punishments and even death. To accomplish this, they endured hardships we cannot even relate to so they could establish themselves in the New World we now called America.

When the ship called the Mayflower, reached the New World almost 400 years ago, they landed in what is now known as Provincetown, Massachusetts on the tip of Cape Cod. Today there is a lovely small park on this site with plaques identifying it as The Pilgrim Landing Park. Before the Pilgrims set foot on this new land, they worked together aboard the ship to create and agree on a charter that they called The Mayflower Compact. This was an agreement written and signed by the men on the ship who would be settling themselves and their families at what they called "New Plymouth." Since it may be a while since you have read the Compact or heard it, I'd like to read it to you now.

> *"IN THE NAME OF GOD, AMEN. We, whose names are underwritten, the Loyal Subjects of our dread Sovereign Lord King James, by the Grace of God, of Great Britain, France and Ireland, King, Defender of the Faith, &c. Having undertaken for the Glory of God, and Advancement of the Christian Faith, and the Honour of our King and Country, a Voyage to plant the first Colony in the northern Parts of Virginia; Do by these Presents, solemnly and mutually, in the Presence of God and one another, covenant and combine ourselves together into a civil Body Politick, for our better Ordering and Preservation, and Furtherance of the Ends aforesaid: And by Virtue hereof do enact, constitute, and frame, such just and equal Laws, Ordinances, Acts, Constitutions and Officers, from time to time, as shall be thought most meet and convenient for the general Good of the Colony; unto which we promise all due Submission and Obedience.*
>
> *"IN WITNESS whereof we have hereunto subscribed our names at Cape-Cod the eleventh of November, in the Reign of our Sovereign Lord King James, of England, France, and Ireland, and of Scotland, Anno Domini; 1620."*

These words are followed by the signatures or "marks" of 41 men. At least one man, James Chilton, died there on the ship while it was docked. He never set a foot on this new land but he knew they had arrived and he lived long enough to sign the Mayflower Compact. His daughter, 7 year old Mary, is said to be the first person to touch American soil when they began exiting the ship. These are the people we should think about and be grateful for as we celebrate their spirit and their courage while we gather with our family and friends around a bountiful table. When you do think of them, please remember the words they chose to begin the Compact. It says, "IN THE NAME OF GOD, AMEN."

Enjoy your holiday preparations and family traditions as you celebrate Thanksgiving Day. Think about its original meaning too. Then, as we approach the Advent season, don't forget to also enjoy the real meaning of Christmas. Remember and celebrate the birth of our Lord and Savior. There are 30 days in November. Why not set aside a few minutes each day as a time of Thanksgiving. In addition to your daily devotional time write down something each day that you are especially thankful for – and with very little effort, you may continue with this project long after the holidays!

Enter his gates with thanksgiving and his courts
with praise; Give thanks to him
and praise his name. For the Lord is good and his love endures
forever; his faithfulness continues through all generations.
Psalm 100:4-5

Telephone

Dear Father,

I just had a phone call! The phone rang and when I answered it and said a questioning "hello?" a friendly voice called me by name and told me she was thinking about me. What a great feeling! I was not only thought about, but she took the time to call and tell me so! We chatted and exchanged news. She had news to share with me and she wanted to know how I was! She not only talked, Lord. She listened!

Do you suppose I could brighten someone's day and make them feel this good too? Do you suppose I could keep this chain unbroken that my friend started? But then, did she start it? Maybe someone called her!

I'm going to do it! I'm going to call someone right now and I'll call her by name and tell her I am thinking about her!

Thank you, Lord, for this good feeling of being cared about! Thank You for bringing me to my friend's mind today and for reminding me to think of others.

Walk in wisdom toward those who are outside,
redeeming the time. Let your speech always be with grace,
seasoned with salt, that you may know how
you ought to answer each one.
Colossians 4:5-6

Light

All through the Bible Jesus makes references in various ways to light and to its effect on us as well as the benefits we can enjoy by being in the light. In Isaiah 45:6-7 God is speaking to Cyrus. Note the present tense in these verses: *"I form the light and create darkness, I bring prosperity and create disaster, I the Lord, do all these things. You heavens above, rain down righteousness; let the clouds shower it down. Let the earth open wide, let salvation spring up, let righteousness grow with it; I, the Lord, have created it."*

As Christians, we are all light-receivers, but how many of us are also reflectors? God gives us the gift of light and expects us to use it by reflecting his promises and his love to others around us. Someone once described light as "a hole in the dark." A candle cannot light itself – it cannot glow until it is lit. As a candle burns, it is consumed. It spreads itself and dissipates into the air around it. This is what Jesus did for us when He was here on earth. He came into the world as a Light and he "burned" or "glowed" and spread Himself to all.

Someone once said they read that houses in ancient Palestine were very dark most of the time because each had only one small window. The only lamp was simply a bowl filled with oil and a floating wick, and it was kept on a lampstand in a prominent place in the house. There weren't any matches in those days, and relighting the lamp was difficult, so lamps were left burning almost all the time. When people left the house, they placed an earthenware bushel measure over the lamp. This allowed it to burn safely while they were away. When they returned, the lamp was immediately uncovered so it could bring light to everyone in the family. Light is a powerful force that pushes back the darkness. But there are places where light will not go. It stops at a closed door, and at a closed heart. It can go just so far.

During Bible times, there was a nightly lighting of the festival lamps to illuminate the temple area. When Jesus said, *"I am the Light of the World"* in John 8:12, he may have been referring to this tradition.

In the book of Philippians Paul tells us we are to live clean, innocent lives as children of God in a dark world full of people who are stubborn and crooked. He tells us to shine among them like beacon lights holding out to them the Word of Life. He goes on to say that the good man walks along in the ever-brightening light of God's favor. Talk to God about this when you pray. Ask Him to show you the hidden corners of your life so you can shine out to others.

In Matthew 5 Jesus says, *"You are the light of the world. A city set on a hill cannot be hid. Nor do men light a lamp and put it under a bushel, but on a stand, and it gives light to all in the house. Let your light so shine before men that they may see your good works and give glory to your Father in heaven."* These same verses were repeated many times during the various funeral and memorial services for former President Ronald Reagan.

Something we must remember here... God's word is not meant to shine ahead of us for miles and miles, lighting our way – He only takes us step by step, pace by pace, and unless we wait for His shining guidance, we will plunge into darkness and stumble. In Psalm 119 He promised us a light to light our way. He did not promise a beam to show us the whole course we are on, but a light for our next step – and then the next one. He'll light it enough to keep us from tripping or falling, but only if we stay on the path He has chosen for us!

Lights are not lights until they are lit or turned on. Until then, they are merely bulbs. They are useless – "lightless lights" if you will. This is much like Christianity. If the person of Christ is not central in our lives, His teachings are an empty darkened shell, or an unlit light. Christ's teachings are meaningless or void without Him. That is just as meaningless as a bulb that will not light because the filament is broken or burned out. If it were not for Christ's incandescent presence shining through our lives by the Holy Spirit, Christianity would be just a dark set of rules – dim adornments against the darkness. It is only when light is thrown on them that the difference can be seen.

Light brings cheer! Light brings encouragement into our lives! The little choices we make every day will chart the course of life we follow. We either choose the path of right or we wander off without the benefit of God's light.

It isn't the darkness that really dampens our spirits amid the hard-going times of life. It's seeing no light at the end of the tunnel that depresses us and makes us lose heart. But remember, there is always light! The sun always shines, even when we cannot see it because of darkness or clouds -- and God is always there, even when we cannot see Him. Remember also, you may be the only "light" a non-Christian sees. In this case, how will you be viewed?

May the Light of God shine in all our hearts giving us knowledge of the glory of God until we come face-to-face and see Him and His light in person!

Let light shine out of darkness. II Corinthians 4:6

Family

—— ∮ ——

LORD, I WAS thinking about the word "family" not long ago. Those 6 little letters say SO much, father. The dictionary says a family is "all the people living in the same house," or "a social unit consisting of parents and their children," or "a group of people related by ancestry or marriage."

You thought a lot about families, too, Lord. You chose to be born into a family so we could identify with You more easily – and probably so You could identify with us too. You had a mother and a father and also a heavenly Father, just as I do. You were guided and led and nurtured by Your parents just as I was by mine, and you also led and taught them, as my children have done and are still doing with me.

Your family was important to You. You even took time as You suffered on the cross to be certain someone would be looking out for Your mother Mary when You were no longer there physically. You wanted to be certain she would have someone else to care for when You were no longer on the scene, and someone to care for her too. That not only paints a beautiful picture for us, Lord, but it is also a beautiful example.

Thank You for my family, Lord; for the ones living in my house, for my parents, for my brother and sister and their families, for my own children and for all others related to me by ancestry or by marriage. Help me to remember that the word "family" also denotes a responsibility. You truly lived up to Yours – now please help me live up to mine!

Abundant Sonshine

For we know that if our earthly house, this tent, is destroyed, we have a building from God, a house not made with hands, eternal in the heavens.
II Corinthians 5:1

Holy Communion

———— § ————

HOLY COMMUNION IS a supper for believers. It is a sacrament in which believers look back thankfully to Jesus' passion and look forward expectantly to His return.

Holy Communion is a giving and a taking. I give God my sins and I take His forgiveness. I give Him my old self and take in His new self. He gives me Himself as I take in his body and blood to merge with my own and become one. This makes me stronger physically because I am giving the bad part of my life away and I am stronger spiritually because I am taking on more of God in my life.

God never stops giving!

Is not the cup of thanksgiving for which we give thanks a
participation in the blood of Christ? And is not the bread that
we break, a participation in the body of Christ?
Because there is one loaf, we who are many, are one body,
for we all partake of the one loaf.
I Corinthians 10:16-17

And when he had given thanks, he broke it and said,
"This is my body, which is for you; do this in remembrance of me."
I Corinthians 11:24

In the same way, after supper he took the cup, saying,
"This cup is the new covenant in my blood; do this,
whenever you drink it, in remembrance of me."
I Corinthians 11:25

Plumb Line

———— ∫ ————

THE DICTIONARY SAYS a plumb or a plumb line is a lead weight hung at the end of a line or rope or on one end of a length of string. It is used to determine how deep water is – or whether a wall, etc. is vertical. It means the area from the top of that piece of line or string to the bottom of the piece of lead is straight up and down – it is absolute. I remember someone suggested I use a plumb line when I was putting ceramic tiles on the wall behind the kitchen stove at our first home – and again when I decided I wanted wallpaper in that same kitchen. I found that piece of string with a small weight on it to be absolutely invaluable to making my tiles straight – and later for the lengths of wallpaper to line up and match. Without that plumb line the tiles and wallpaper could easily have been crooked and out of line and it would have been obvious to all who came to my home that I was a novice and I had made a serious mistake.

Today, we can think of God as being <u>our</u> plumb line. He's there, at the center of our lives, helping us focus and "stay straight." We may find ourselves shifting or leaning a bit to left or right at times, but by turning back to that plumb line, we align ourselves with God and with His teachings.

In the Book of Hebrews, Chapter 12, the writer says, *"Therefore, strengthen your feeble arms and weak knees. Make level paths for your feet so that the lame may not be disabled, but rather healed."* The explanation of these verses says it is a call for upright conduct that will help, rather than hinder, the spiritual and moral welfare of others, especially the "lame" who may waver in their Christian faith.

Let's remember this: it is difficult to see the straightness of the line if you are not looking straight at it – and it's the same with God. We find it awkward to try and look to God if we are just looking at Him out of the corner of an eye. We need to be facing Him straight on. We need to stand tall and align ourselves with Him because He offers Himself as a plumb line to each of us.

Let your eyes look straight ahead, fix your gaze directly before you.
Make level paths for your feet and take only ways that are firm.
Do not swerve to the right or the left.
Prov. 4:25-27

Automobiles

———— ◊ ————

JUST FOR A moment, clear your minds and think about an automobile in relation to the human body and to our Christian walk – or should I say ride? Anyway, while we do that, let's think of God as our first-class mechanic. He knows all of our parts and our fittings, no matter what model we are, or how many miles we may have on our chassis. God is an excellent repairman and He can break us (or <u>brake</u> us) and He can repair us, or patch us up so we can at least get by, or, when He feels the time is right, He can put us out of commission permanently.

We each have an owners' manual and that is the Bible. This manual has all the answers we need to keep ourselves in good operating condition. Our headlights are really the Holy Spirit who lights the path before us – either on low beam or high beam - so we can see better, both in daytime and in darkness. Our power base is made up of our engine and our transmission. The transmission is our wisdom which gives us power. Our steering wheel helps to keep us on the straightaway, or to turn right or left when it is necessary to alter our path. You might say we have Power steering with a capital P!

All automobiles have an exhaust system. The intake valve lets the fuel mixture flow into the cylinder and the exhaust valve allows the burned gases to escape out through the tailpipe. Joy could be said to be our pressure – and praise is the safety valve letting it go outward! Joy is inward – praise is outward.

The generator or the regulator protects the electrical system from damage by excessive voltage. This could be called our repentance which involves a change of attitude, a change in our thinking and then a change in our outlook.

Cars have batteries to keep them going. These batteries stabilize the voltage in our electrical systems by having a positive and a negative pole. The negative pole grounds us to the frame of the car while the positive pole runs to the motor. Our relationship with God is our battery. We should ground ourselves in a realistic awareness of our limitations while we move forward with positive possibilities. Our self-esteem is based upon our recognition of these positive and negative poles. When we cease to have a relationship with God, our batteries die and when they do, they must either be recharged or replaced.

The tires on a car, when properly inflated, offer us a nice smooth ride. Four of them are required to keep the car balanced. Forgiveness, goodness, justice and mercy can offer us a well-balanced life. Air pressure must be maintained or the ride can become bumpy. A slow leak – or worse yet, a blowout, - can wreck a car – or a life.

Cars must have good brakes. The safety of many depends on a reliable, well-functioning brake system. Self-control is the Christian's brake system. The seats and seat belts in our car offer comfort and safety – and God offers us these same things through His Son, Jesus, as our loving Savior.

Gasoline and oil, like God, are there to keep our parts in motion so we must never let the parts go dry. The oil could also refer to our prayer life as it lubricates and helps us function.

The gears on the car could equate to our conversion when we come to God. He helps us change directions so we go in the right direction, where He wants us to be.

Parking spaces for automobiles can be very evasive. Many cars – and people – go around in circles looking for just the right one – but as Christians, each of us has a special place in heaven and it is already marked "reserved"!

Take good care of your personal automobile while you are on your Christian walk (or ride) and your trip will be much smoother and ever so much more rewarding in the end!

Grace and peace be yours in abundance
through the knowledge of God and of Jesus our Lord.
II Peter 1:2

Sunshine

———— § ————

Dear Lord,

The sun is shining today! It is so bright and beautiful as it rises over the roof of the house across the street and shines here and beyond. You gave Your Son to be OUR dazzling light. What a glorious gift and how we thank you! Each time the sun comes up, it is a reminder of the aura that must have been around Jesus as He walked from town to town. There is magnetism about the sunlight. We can see that in the dust particles that dance and lift themselves in its rays. It is so bright we cannot look directly at it!

Jesus has magnetism too! His light draws us near to Him and shuts away the threat of darkness. He lightens and enlightens us and makes us want to lift ourselves and our thoughts to Him.

The sun moves around the sky throughout the day and night, but it is always there, even on cloudy days, and it is for each one of us to enjoy and to use. Sometimes it is hard to see it because of the clouds, but we can still find comfort in knowing it is there.

Jesus is always there, too, aren't you, Lord? We cannot always see You and maybe we don't always feel Your presence, but You are there! Maybe sometimes it is I who is hiding....

Abundant Sonshine

The Lord is my light and my salvation – whom shall I fear?
The Lord is the stronghold of my life – of whom shall I be afraid?
Psalm 27:1

Certificate

—— § ——

Soon after we are born here in America, paperwork and information are submitted and we are then issued a Birth Certificate by the government of the State in which we were born. This certificate proves we were born and it gives various statistics about our height and weight at birth, our parentage, etc. A little later, when we are baptized, we receive a Baptismal Certificate from the church or clergy responsible for performing this rite. If we complete classes about our church and our religion choices, we may become confirmands and then we receive a Certificate of Confirmation or Certificate of Membership. Upon the completion of the required educational classes, at least in the United States, we receive a Diploma after our twelfth year of schooling and this shows we have met certain educational requirements and we were eligible to be graduated. We may then choose to go on for more schooling, in which case we may receive Certificates for the degrees of all advanced study we elect to pursue.

When two people marry, they receive a Marriage Certificate showing them to be husband and wife. Later – much later, we hope! – we will cease to live and breathe, and then an official Death Certificate is issued indicating the time, date and place we died along with the cause of our death.

For something to be certified it must be true and accurate. These documents I just mentioned must be signed – and sometimes witnessed – by a person or persons in charge or by someone with authority. Many times they will also have an official "seal" on these documents. They are certifying that these events did happen as stated and many people will frame these documents and display them proudly, or they will keep them in a safe place so they are available if needed for verification of any kind in the future.

We don't have anything directly from God to indicate we are His children, but we know from the Bible that He knows everything about us – from even before our birth while we are still in the womb, until well after our death and our burial or cremation, signifying our departure from this world. He keeps track of our comings and our goings – of our good deeds and our lack of good deeds, and the Psalmist David tells us that God saves our tears in a bottle with our name on it. Each of us is important to Him – even our tears! And let us not forget that each of us is also accountable to Him.

Let's each mentally create our own Certificate of Belonging as a reminder that we are indeed children of God and that we do belong to Him. Let's mentally frame this document reminding us that we have met the requirements by accepting Jesus as our Lord and Savior, and we are now officially designated as a child of God and we belong to Him!

> *The Spirit himself testifies with our spirit that we are God's children.*
> *Now if we are children, then we are heirs – heirs of God and*
> *co-heirs with Christ, if indeed we share in his sufferings*
> *in order that we may also share in his glory.*
> *Romans 8:16, 17*

Potter

—— § ——

A POTTER IS a person who makes earthenware vessels. Part of the explanation in the encyclopedia says the art of pottery goes way back in history. Numerous historical periods are cited when different types of pottery were found during archeological digs. Well, I found you can go back even <u>farther</u> because the potter and pottery are mentioned in the Bible. Isaiah made a reference to reducing clay to paste when he said this in Isaiah 41:25, *"I have stirred up one from the north, and he comes — one from the rising sun who calls on my name. He treads on rulers as if they were mortar, as if he were a potter treading the clay."* Later, in Jeremiah 18:1 Jeremiah said the Lord told him to go to the potter's house where he would receive a message. This not only confirms that a potter was a profession, but it also indicates a specific place to do this work. Jeremiah went on to say the pot the potter was shaping from clay was marred in his hands; so the potter formed it into another pot, shaping it as seemed best to him. Jeremiah 18:6 says the Lord spoke to him and said, *"Like clay in the hand of the potter, so are you in my hand, O house of Israel."*

Did you notice that Jeremiah did not say the potter tried to <u>fix</u> the marred pot, or smooth over it to cover the flaw? He said the potter formed it into another pot. He broke it down and he reworked it. The clay a potter works with must yield itself to the potter's touch. The potter <u>never</u> takes his eyes off the clay while he's working with it. He must be constantly alert for flaws so they can be corrected immediately before the flaw has a chance to grow and become permanent and even more noticeable. While he is working with a piece of clay, the potter keeps his work swathed in a protective damp cloth overnight so the clay will not dry out. In this way he keeps it pliant and yielding – utterly surrendered to his will and to his touch. He always has a plan and things must be completed in a certain order to become the finished product he envisions.

When God recognizes our flaws, instead of discarding us, He reshapes us and our lives. He keeps the mold moving, He waters us down, and never taking His hands or His eyes off of us, He reworks us. In this way, He makes us more usable – more acceptable in His sight. This process can serve to point us in another direction – HIS direction!

Sometimes we may feel like we are useless and flawed. We are covered in a damp cloth and it may be difficult to see that as being protective, but it is. When God reshapes us and reworks us, our flaws and impurities disappear and we become stronger physically, mentally and emotionally. We must remember that God knows what He is doing in each of us. He is the potter, and we are His clay. He has a plan for each of us and He will mold us and make us and expose us to just enough pressures of just the right kinds that we may be made into a flawless piece of work to fulfill His good, pleasing and perfect will.

If life seems hard at times and you feel you're being pounded, patted and pushed almost beyond endurance – when your world seems to be spinning out of control – when you feel like you are in a fiery furnace of trials, try this remedy: Brew a cup of your favorite tea, pour it into your prettiest teacup, sit down and have a little talk with The Potter!

"Yet, O Lord, you are our Father.
We are the clay, you are the potter; we are all the work of your hand."
Isaiah 64:8

Marriage and Music

Marriage and music have much in common.
Each can run smoothly and melodic as in a quiet ballad.
Sometimes there's rock and roll,
or jazz with its loud noises and ups and downs.
Some music may be sad and blue
while others can be a romantic rhapsody.

To make memorable music or a lasting marriage
all instruments must be in tune and keep the same rhythm.
Both take practice, patience, endurance, plus devotion
and forgiveness and move on.

Then, with smoothly flowing tones,
You will experience a satisfaction
not only in pleasing yourself,
but also your mate and others around you.

Temptation

TEMPTATION IS SOMETHING we cannot avoid in our lives. We are faced with various forms of temptation each day, beginning with the very moment we awake! Nowhere in the Bible does it say we can escape temptation, nor does it say that temptation in itself is wrong. The right or wrong of temptation becomes evident in our response to it. Our decision to give in to it makes it wrong, and each time we avoid it and reject it, we are built up both emotionally and spiritually.

Luke says temptations to sin are sure to come. James refers to temptations and trials being part of our lives. He speaks of <u>when</u> we are tempted, not <u>if</u>. And he stresses that when we give way to it, no one else can be blamed. We had a choice – we always do!

Satan, in the form of a serpent, planted a thought in Eve's mind. He implied that God was withholding something good from her by telling her not to eat of the tree of the knowledge of good and evil. Satan convinced her she would be more like God if she ate of that tree. Then she would know everything HE knew. In one way, Satan was right. After eating of it and tempting another to do the same, she, like God, could distinguish between good and evil. The difference is she carried this new knowledge by sinning while God remained pure. Along with her new knowledge, she acquired a conscience – a guilty one! She immediately realized her vulnerability to sin and its effects on her body and mind and she tried to hide and covered herself with a fig leaf.

God, through the sacrifice of His Son Jesus, has provided us with a more protective covering than a mere, tiny fig leaf. He offers us His huge robe of righteousness when we come to Him and admit our sinfulness by asking for His forgiveness. He also offers us the Holy Spirit who, when dwelling in us, can enable us to refuse temptations.

We tend to see temptation as a test of will power. God sees it as a test of faith. He will not remove trials and temptations from our lives. We need these to help us grow. However, when we are tempted, we need to remind ourselves that the long-term pain of giving in will far outweigh any momentary pleasure. Lot's wife gave in to temptation and she became a pillar of salt!

Try this: Picture yourself dressed in a fig leaf which will soon wither and die. Then picture yourself clothed in Christ's beautiful robe of righteousness. Which one would you rather wear?

"Be self-controlled and alert. Your enemy the devil prowls around like a roaring lion looking for someone to devour. Resist him, standing firm in the faith, because you know that your brothers throughout the world are undergoing the same kind of sufferings."
I Peter 5:8, 9

Wisdom

THE DICTIONARY DESCRIBES wisdom as *"the quality of being wise; using good judgment based on knowledge; wise teaching."* My Bible Concordance says it is *"knowledge guided by understanding."* In the Bible, the Book of Proverbs has much to say on the subject of wisdom. It starts in Chapter 1 by saying that *"the fear of the Lord is the beginning of knowledge"* – and it goes on to say that fools despise wisdom. Proverbs 3:13-14 says *"Blessed is the man who finds wisdom, the man who gains understanding, for he is more profitable than silver and yields better returns than gold."* In that same chapter we are told we should have two goals: wisdom and common sense, both of which mean knowing and doing right. The Living Bible says these things will fill you with living energy and they are a feather in your cap. A few chapters later, in Proverbs 8, we are advised to *"Choose my instruction instead of silver, knowledge rather than choice gold, for Wisdom is more precious than rubies, and nothing you desire can compare with her."* Later, in Chapter 28 we are told that *"he who walks in wisdom is kept safe."*

Proverbs 31 emphasizes the role and significance of wise women. Verses 10 to 31 describe a woman who fears the Lord. (The explanatory notes in my NIV Bible say that these verses are also an acrostic because each verse begins with a successive letter of the Hebrew alphabet.) These verses describe a wife of noble character and they go on to say she is clothed with strength and dignity; she is free of anxiety and worry; she is a wise and loving counselor and her joy radiates to others. What a challenge and a positive role model this presents for women today!

James 3:17 says *"Wisdom that is from above is pure, peaceable, gentle, easy to be entreated, full of mercy, full of good fruits, without partiality, and without hypocrisy."* The Amplified version goes on to say it is "full of compassion; wholehearted; straight-forward. Another version of the Bible uses the phrases "peace-loving, considerate, and submissive." In Ecclesiastes 8:1 it says that *"Wisdom brightens a man's face and changes its hard appearance."*

Luke 2 says that as a child, Jesus grew and became strong and he was filled with wisdom, and the grace of God was upon Him. Later in Chapter 21 Jesus says *"For I will give you words and wisdom that none of your adversaries will be able to resist or contradict."* In I Corinthians 2 we are told that God revealed wisdom to man through His Spirit.

I once read that there are 35 synonyms for wisdom, but there is NO substitute for it! I also read that wisdom is the difference between pulling your weight and throwing it around! True wisdom always starts with a heart full of faith, not a head full of facts.

We can <u>want</u> wisdom – we can even <u>wish</u> for wisdom – but true wisdom is a gift from God and one to be treasured above all else. James tells us to ask God for it because God always gives generously to all. Remember, true wisdom starts with a heart full of faith, not a head full of facts.

I saw that wisdom is better than folly, just
as light is better than darkness.
Ecclesiastes 2:13

Eyes

LORD, IF MY eyes are on YOU, they won't be on ME. I seem to have too much ME in my life some days and I want more of YOU instead. Help me to sharpen my focus and to open my heart and my eyes as you lead and instruct my life for Your glory. I am renewed because of You, Lord. I have a new life because You gave Yours for me – even me! Strengthen and deepen my love and my trust as I walk with You. Help me to use myself to my fullest potential. Keep my goals set high and my eyes set on You as I go through each day.

After all – I am a Child of God!

Keep your eyes on Jesus, our leader and instructor. Hebrews 12:2a (LB)

Beatitudes for Today

———— § ————

HERE IS ANOTHER version of the Beatitudes – a variation in what we might call "plainer English." The author is unknown.

In Matthew 5:3-12 -- God is speaking to everyone:

> Happy are the humble-minded, for the kingdom of Heaven is theirs.
> Happy are those who know what sorrow means for they will be given courage and comfort.
> Happy are those who claim nothing, for the whole earth will belong to them.
> Happy are those who hunger and thirst for goodness, for they will be fully satisfied.
> Happy are the utterly sincere, for they will surely see God.
> Happy are those who make peace, for they will be sons of God.
> Happy are those who have suffered persecution for the cause of goodness, for the
> Kingdom of Heaven is theirs.
> What happiness will be yours when people blame you and ill-treat you or say slanderous things against you for my sake. Be glad then; yes, be tremendously goad, for your reward in Heaven is magnificent!

In Luke 6:20b-23a -- God is speaking to you:

How happy are you who own nothing for the kingdom of God is yours.

How happy are you who are hungry now, for you will be satisfied.

How happy are you who week now, for you are going to laugh.

How happy you are when men hate you and turn you out of their company; when they slander you and detest all that you stand for because you are loyal to the Son of Man. Be glad when that happens and jump for joy – your reward in Heaven is magnificent!

In John 15:10-11 -- God is speaking to you:

If you keep my commandments you will live in my love just as I have kept my Father's commandments and live in His love. I have told you this so that you can share my joy, and that your happiness may be complete!

In Romans 12:12 -- God is challenging you:

Base your happiness on your hope in Christ! Share the happiness of those who are happy! If anyone is flourishing (or happy) let him sing praises to God!

Up North

THERE IS A family resort in the woods on a lake in far northern Wisconsin that my family has enjoyed visiting several times over the last few years. Meals are served in the Main Lodge and one evening I wandered around admiring all the pictures on the walls. One particular framed poem caught my attention and I found myself thinking of it many times during our visit that summer. I'm not sure who wrote it but here is what it says:

UP NORTH

There's a lot of talk about "up north" … It's the place everyone seems to want to go to escape the pressures and frantic pace of everyday life. But where IS "up north"?

If you ask a dozen people, you'll get that many answers. For "up north" is not so much a location as it is a state of mind. So, how do you know when you've arrived "up north"?

It's when you feel the cares of the world begin to slip away … It's when you feel your- self breathing a little deeper because the air seems purer somehow… When you notice that the sky looks bluer, the water is clearer, the trees stand taller, and the people smile a lot…

Then you know you are "UP NORTH"!

Where is YOUR "up north?" Stop and think about these words for a minute. For some, "up north" might be sitting in their favorite chair with a good book while enjoying a fresh cup of coffee or tea, or a glass of wine. For some, it might be pushing a child or grandchild on a swing and listening to them giggle and laugh with excitement. For others, it might be some favorite verses or chapters in the Bible that always seem to calm them and help them set the world aside for a short time so they can bask in the promises and words of Jesus. Maybe you feel you are "up north" when you take a walk on a summer's day and hear the birds and feel a gentle breeze around you. Or maybe it's enjoying a card game with friends.

Your "up north" can change often throughout your lifetime. There was a time years ago when my "up north" started when my husband came through the door after a long day at work. We moved to the country, I had a new baby and no car, it was winter, and I had no opportunity to meet any neighbors – and it was a long distance call to call my family or friends. When I heard his key in the door, I took a deep breath, I smiled and rushed to greet him, and my "up north" was then all around me. His day was ending and mine was just beginning!

At another time of my life, "up north" meant family members coming to visit from another state. When my parents or siblings, nieces and nephews crowded around our dining room table and their many voices and laughter filled the air, I was suddenly transported "up north."

Let us not forget that God is our "up north" ALL the time! We only need to pause and think about Him, or speak to Him in prayer, or read His Word, and then we truly are "up north!"

Patience and Impatience

———— § ————

Heavenly Father,

You have so much to say to us in the Bible about patience. I'm so glad You are patient with me! You never seem to be irritated with me for my negligence or my uncaring acts or my forgetfulness. When I ask for forgiveness you are quick to give it. I am sometimes quick to look to You for a pat on the back when I think I've done something nice – but I'm not so quick to admit I repeated something told me in confidence – or that I ate cookies when I knew I shouldn't – or I put off studying my Bible lesson or reading my daily devotions. I am often inclined to rush into situations without first consulting You – and that's a little like trying to prepare a gourmet meal without any recipes! All I wind up with is a mess and nothing to show for it but frazzle and frustration! Help me to be more appreciative of Your patience with me.

You give us so many examples of your patience. I think particularly about David – and Peter – and Jacob – and Paul. Each one lacked patience at some point and went ahead on their own, but You did not abandon them or turn Your back on any of them. You helped each one turn his life around and get back on Your track. Jeremiah told about the potter who found a flaw in a piece he had molded. Instead of discarding it and starting with new clay, he broke the imperfect piece down and lovingly started over and patiently reworked it until it turned out just as he had envisioned it. That's what You do for us, too, Father, and it's all done with such love! Thank you again for Your patience!

Amen

II Peter 3:15 "Bear in mind that our Lord's patience means salvation."

Colossians 1:11 "Be strengthened with all power according to his glorious might so that you may have great endurance and patience, and joyfully giving thanks to the Father, who has qualified you to share in the inheritance of the saints in the kingdom of light."

Water

As PLANTS OR gardens require water to grow, to live and to survive, we humans, too, need water to exist. We need the wet kind of water to swallow and to nourish our physical bodies, and we also need watering from God's Word on a regular basis or else our soul and our life can become dry and brittle due to spiritual neglect. We need our Bibles, we need prayer, and we need Christian fellowship to feed us and to feed our souls.

Water is mentioned in the Bible at least 464 times according to a Bible Concordance. There are 400 references to it in the Old Testament and 64 references in the New Testament. Water is referred to 32 times in the book of Genesis. This is more often than in any other book of the Bible. Next is the book of Numbers where water is mentioned 30 times.

In the Concordance, water is referred to as "a colorless liquid that can be used to moisten or be sprinkled". Water is said to create, to bless the earth, to be living, to be cold, to be deep, and to be mighty. It can be used for drinking, for washing, for vegetation, for cleansing, for ordination, for purification, for sanctification, and for baptism. Water is an essential part of the Rite of Baptism because it signifies our renewal and our dedication to God.

In Genesis, God created the waters of the earth and called them seas – and he created many species of fish to live in the waters. Also in Genesis, water flooded the earth, but this same water bore up the ark and all its inhabitants who were saved. In Exodus, young Moses was put into a basket by his mother who feared for his life. This basket was put into the Nile River where it floated until he was found by Pharaoh's daughter who then raised him. Later, in Exodus Chapter 14, at God's command, Moses raised his staff over the Red Sea and the waters were parted allowing the Israelites to cross to safety, and the waters of this same sea then crushed and killed the Egyptians who had been pursuing them.

John the Baptist baptized hundreds in the River Jordan and said this was done for repentance. He went on to say that he baptized with water but the one who was to come after him would be more powerful and He would baptize with the Holy Spirit. Then Jesus came from Galilee to the Jordan where He was baptized by John.

At the beginning of His ministry Jesus changed water into wine at the wedding in Cana. This was the first of His many miracles. Later, He met the Samaritan woman at Jacob's Well and asked her to draw water for him to drink, and then He told her He was the Living Water. He went on to say that whoever drinks of this Living Water will never thirst. Jesus also used water for healing and later, when He was with His disciples on the Sea of Galilee, He walked on water.

Jesus used water to wash the feet of the disciples at the Last Supper just prior to His arrest and His crucifixion. Afterward He told them he was doing this as an example of humble service so that later, in carrying out his ministry, they would do as He had done and not set themselves above anyone.

Today, water is an essential part of our rite of baptism. We are baptized with water in the name of God the Father, God the Son, and God the Holy Spirit as we are committed to God. Although this may not be a physical cleansing, it is a form of spiritual cleansing and this rite or ritual is considered sacred.

When we water our lawns, we don't pour all the water in one place. We sprinkle it around so ALL of the lawn can benefit and be nourished. Many people use sprinklers that oscillate or they may even have a special automatic sprinkling system. Let's think of ourselves as a sprinkler for God! Let's oscillate and pour forth His Word, His love, and His commands in all that we do and say so we can cover all directions.

"The fruit of the righteous is a tree of life,
and he who wins souls is wise."
Proverbs 11:30

Interruptions

THE WORDS INTERRUPTIONS and opportunities each have 13 letters. Ruth Bell Graham, the wife of evangelist Billy Graham, once said that interruptions never distracted Jesus. He accepted them as opportunities for a time of richer service.

Many of the interruptions mentioned in the Bible were merely people who were seeking Jesus' help. I've listed just a few:

(1) The Canaanite woman on her knees who wanted the scraps from the table in Matthew 15.
(2) The violent, demon-possessed man in Mark 5 who begged Jesus to drive out his demons.
(3) Blind Bartimaeus, in Mark 10 who wanted his sight restored.
(4) The leper in Matthew 8 who wanted to be cleansed.
(5) The centurion in Matthew 8 whose beloved servant was dying but Jesus healed him.
(6) The paralytic who had himself lowered through a roof to be in Jesus' presence in Mark 2 because he wanted to walk again.
(7) The bleeding woman who only wished to touch His garment in hopes of being healed in Matthew 9.

These are only a few "interruptions" that are mentioned in the Bible. Jesus used each one as an opportunity. In each situation, Jesus, in His own compassionate way, healed, cured or cleansed the people, not to demonstrate His power, but to demonstrate God's love and Jesus' purpose for coming to live among us.

Here is a prayer I wrote about an interruption when my daughter was a sophomore in high school: *"Well, You've done it again, Lord! You planned something unexpected for my day, and although I thought it was just a nuisance at the time, You showed me how important it was. I had my day all planned, Lord, with little time to spare. Then I found I had to squeeze in a trip to the eye doctor to pick up her new glasses. At first I must admit I resented that intrusion, Lord, but later I was so thankful for it! We had time to talk as I drove and once again as we sat in the waiting room. She needed me for a while, and she needed me as more than a chauffeur. She needed a listener and I needed a breather and you accomplished <u>both</u> with that one "interruption." Times like this are so beautiful and meaningful to look back on at the end of the day, Lord. Help me to appreciate these times more! There really are very few nuisances in my days if I just take the time to see them for the lovely interruptions they can be. Your timing is always SO perfect! Thank You, Loving Father!"*

The next time you feel annoyed about an interruption in your schedule or routine, stop and think. Perhaps this interruption is intended to be an opportunity! Ask yourself what God is trying to tell you or to show you!

"Daughter, your faith has healed you. Go in peace and
be freed from your suffering."
Mark 5:54

Ornaments

———— ✦ ————

AN ORNAMENT IS described as an embellishment or decoration, something that adds luster to its surroundings. The word ornate, which stems from the word ornament, means to be over adorned, or to be showy or flowery. Again, we are describing an external display – something to be viewed by many.

We put ornaments in and around our homes at holiday time, and we put them on our Christmas trees to make them more attractive, beautiful and sparkling. Ornaments are generally intended to attract attention to the tree. They can be of any size or color, or combination of colors. They can be homemade or handmade. They can be cast from metal molds or blown from glass, painted, glazed, enameled, or gilded in gold or silver. They can be large or small because size is not important unless you are decorating with a specific theme in mind.

The tradition of trees and ornaments is a much disputed one and there are several theories about their origins. One article I read said Saint Boniface, the Apostle of the Germans, started the tradition of trees when he came to Germany in the 7th century to preach. He brought a tree for the people to decorate and he claimed its triangular shape represented the Holy Trinity – God, Jesus and the Holy Spirit. This tradition was soon lapped up by the devout Germans who began decorating the trees in a liturgical way with simple white candles. Later, in the 15th century, ornaments began to be incorporated into the Christmas decorations and traditions in Germany.

Another historical record I found says the custom of decorating Christmas trees emerged in the early 16th century in Germany. Martin Luther is credited with decorating the first Christmas tree with candles to entertain the children. During Luther's lifetime Christmas trees began to be embellished with wafers, candies, fruits, paper flowers, hard cookies baked in various shapes, and tinsels made from tin and silver.

Time passed, and in the early 1800's trees began to be decorated with edible items such as fruit (especially apples) and nuts because these were the items that would grow on trees. Later paper streamers and bits of shiny metal foil were used. Then the idea of reflecting the light into the room came into being. Another tradition began about this time – foods like gingerbread and hard cookies baked in varying shapes such as fruits, stars, bells, hearts, angels, etc., were used as decorations.

As the tradition of Christmas trees and ornaments became more widespread, each country added its own ingenuity to the decorations. For example, the Americans began stringing long strands of cranberries and popcorn to encircle their trees. As America took more and more to this new tradition, a man named F. W. Woolworth, a retailer, began selling imported glass ornaments in his shops starting about 1880. It's been said that by 1890 he sold $25 million of them. Remember, Woolworth's was a Five & Dime Store, so that's a lot of ornaments!

The First World War disrupted natural commerce and this necessitated the production of cheaper ornaments and required finding new technologies. In the United Kingdom, imaginative ornaments of lace and paper showed the ingenuity and skill of their makers. Then, thin foil strips, better known today as icicles or tinsel, began to be created in Germany and they found much favor all over the world because of their reflective quality.

During Queen Victoria's reign, glass ornaments and decorative glass beads began to be used. Soon small gifts began to be hung on the trees, sometimes tucked into little baskets which were nestled in the crook of a branch or suspended by small pieces of thread. In fact, so many decorative items began to be used during this period that with each passing year it became increasingly difficult to actually see the tree because of the ornaments!

German entrepreneurs in the late 1800's began thinking of manufacturing ornaments on a mass scale and selling them strictly as Christmas ornaments. Glass firms which had previously made only bottles and marbles began to create little glass toy molds shaped like saints, famous people, animals, etc. They were well received and special factories and foundries sprang up as these individually crafted ornaments became highly prized possessions.

Early in the 20th century Germany had somewhat of a monopoly but since 1925 Japan has challenged that dominance by producing ornaments on a large scale. They brought in newer, more colorful designs. Later the Czech Republic entered this competition with an impressive amount of fancy ornaments. By 1935, more than 250 million Christmas tree ornaments were being imported to America. Still, Germany retained a solid market base the world over because of the originality in their handicraft. Many were all handmade, often by people who followed ancestral glass making traditions.

During World War I a U.S. businessman persuaded the Corning Glass Company in New York become involved in this business and they invented special machinery that could mass-produce these ornaments which were then sent to other companies to be decorated. One of these machines is now displayed at the Henry Ford Museum near Dearborn, Michigan.

Next Christmas, as you decorate your tree, think a bit about some of these old traditions that started it all. Most of all I would challenge you to remember that the original tree was intended as a visual reminder of the Holy Trinity – God, Jesus and the Holy Spirit!

Cynthia Irish Hockins

May the grace of the Lord Jesus Christ, and the love of God,
and the fellowship of the Holy Spirit be with you all.
II Corinthians 13:14

Forgiveness

THE DICTIONARY SAYS that forgiveness is a form of pardon. When you truly forgive, you not only overlook the problem, you also give up the resentment accompanying it. You cancel that debt. A Bible Concordance says forgiveness is the act of pardoning.

Jesus spoke often about forgiveness in the New Testament. In Matthew Chapter 6, where Jesus tells his disciples how to pray, he says when we ask to have our sins forgiven, we must also be prepared to forgive any who may have sinned against us. By doing this, He says, our heavenly Father will forgive us. To make it even more clear and to leave no room for doubt, he says in verse 15 that if we do not forgive our fellow men their sins, our Father in Heaven will not forgive <u>our</u> sins. From that, I have to conclude that forgiveness is a two-way street.

In Acts 2, Peter tells the people to repent and be baptized in the name of Jesus Christ for the forgiveness of your sins and you will receive the gift of the Holy Spirit. When Jesus spoke to his disciples in Luke 17, He said, *"If your brother sins, rebuke him, and if he repents, forgive him. If he sins against you seven times a day, and seven times comes back to you and says, 'I repent,' forgive him."*

There are numerous examples of forgiveness all through the Old Testament. Two outstanding examples are given in Genesis where we read that Esau forgave Jacob for stealing his birthright and later Joseph forgave his brothers for selling him into slavery. In the New Testament in Acts 7, as Stephen was being stoned to death because he was a follower, his last words were, *"Lord, do not hold this sin against them."* But the greatest example of forgiveness, the forgiveness of all forgivenesses, was uttered by Jesus Himself as he hung on the cross. He said, *"Father forgive them, for they do not know what they are doing."*

> *Forgive us our debts, as we also have forgiven our debtors.*
> *Matthew 6:12*

Aging
Ready or not...

———— § ————

GROWING OLDER SHOULD be viewed as a privilege and not a penalty. In fact, there are many dividends to aging. In what is often referred to as "retirement," we have the opportunity to cultivate friendships that may have long been neglected due to work and family commitments. We also have the opportunity to witness unhurriedly by our deeds and our actions – and these opportunities often cross generational lines as we deal with younger people. These younger ones may be relatives or even the strangers we encounter during our daily living. We have a chance to serve both our church and our community and to offer the benefits of some of our life experiences. Another benefit is that we have more time for prayer!

Through the years I've made some notes on aging and I recorded a few quotes by writers, etc., but in checking in my Bible Concordance, I was pleased to see many mentions of aging are listed in the Bible. I checked some of them out to see what God tells us about this period in our lives. The Concordance broke it down into several categories. It refers to the handicaps of age, the glories of age, and the attitude of others toward age.

Under handicaps, in Genesis, after Joseph was reunited with his brothers and his father, it says Jacob's eyes were failing because of old age so Joseph brought his two children up close to him so Jacob might embrace them and hold them. We, too, often experience changes in our eyesight but today we are blessed with eye doctors who are trained to evaluate our problems and they are often able to correct them for us, at least partially if not totally. In Psalm 71 the Psalmist David prays asking for God's help in his old age when enemies threaten because they can see that the king's strength is waning. Our physical strength decreases as we age, too, but again, God often provides help for us through trained personnel and therapists, through wheel chairs, walkers, braces, canes, etc. In Ecclesiastes Chapter 12 there are several verses referring to our deterioration in our old age. It says our eyes may grow dim, our hands and feet may tremble, we may experience problems with our teeth and our ears and our hair, but this is all unimportant if we are still able to remember our Creator and honor Him and keep His commandments in a spirit of love and worship.

Now let's think about the *glories* of aging! In the book of Job he says, "Is not wisdom found among the aged? Does not long life bring understanding?" Proverbs 31 reminds us that gray hair is a crown of splendor and it is attained by a righteous life. I like to think I'm becoming more splendid every day! In Leviticus the Lord is giving instructions to Moses to pass along to the people of Israel. He says, "Rise in the presence of the aged, show respect for the elderly and revere your God." In Luke 2 Simeon was rewarded in his old age when the child Jesus was brought to the Temple and Simeon took him in his arms and recognized him as the fulfillment of God's promises. He then said he was ready to be dismissed, or to die, because he had seen the salvation of God who was to be a light to the Gentiles and a glory to the people of Israel.

In our maturing years, we should constantly remember that time may wrinkle our skin but it cannot wrinkle our soul. We should also remember that our energy level is often more a matter of our attitude than our age. In order to stay sharp we must remain socially active because the ones who withdraw are the ones who tend to decline rapidly. We should keep mentally active because this will increase our intellectual acuity. We must be flexible – how often have we each learned THAT lesson! When we are flexible, I think it encourages our mental alertness. And above all, we should practice a positive attitude.

During my husband's last months in the nursing home, any time he was asked how he was doing or how he was feeling, no matter <u>how</u> he felt his reply was to smile and say he felt "fantastic!" This always made people smile back at him and people came to expect and enjoy his good attitude. He told me in private that no one wanted to hear his complaints so why dwell on them unnecessarily. He was happiest when he made someone else smile! Several of his nursing home caretakers contacted me after his death to say how much they missed him and his wonderful smile and good attitude.

Old age – (or maturity, which sounds much better) -- should be regarded as a reward for a lifetime of hard work. A writer once said it can only be considered a punishment if one insists on doing the same things one has always done, and in the same manner it's always been done, measuring present achievements by past ones, and inevitably falling short.

I wish you a <u>fantastic</u> day!!

Two Men

—— § ——

OH, HEAVENLY FATHER, in one chapter of Your book, the Bible, I read of two men who sought You. Both came close enough to speak to you in spite of pressing crowds around You, and each pushed forward to get closer because they had questions and concerns.

The rich young ruler asked for eternal life, but would not give up his earthly wealth and riches to attain it. He kept his wealth and lost the gift of eternal life. He left Your presence feeling very sad. On the other hand, Bartimaeus was a blind beggar who owned only the cloak on his back. When You agreed to talk to him, he cast even that cloak aside and hurried to You with his request for sight that he might see You.

Bartimaeus gained SO much more than just his sight, Father. He gained riches untold because he gained far more than worldly wealth! He gained the riches of heaven!

Father, when I am tempted by worldly things and blinded by things around me, help me to remember those two men and the choices they made. Help me to make the right choice, and to "cast off" my cloak and run to You!

Abundant Sonshine

If anyone would come after me, he must
deny himself and take up his cross
and follow me. For whoever wants to save his life will lose it,
but whoever loses his life for me will find it.
What good will it be for a man if he gains the
whole world, yet forfeits his soul?
Matthew 16:24

Isaiah

———— ◊ ————

The Book of Isaiah mirrors the whole Bible

THERE ARE 66 chapters in the book of Isaiah and there are 66 books in the Bible

The book of Isaiah is divided into 2 parts and the Bible also has two parts: the Old Testament and the New Testament.

The Bible has 39 books in the Old Testament and 27 books in the New Testament.

It has been said that the first 39 chapters of Isaiah and the Old Testament both deal with judgment, and the last 27 chapters of Isaiah and the 27 books in the New Testament all deal with comfort.

So do not fear, for I am with you; do not be dismayed for
I am your God. I will strengthen you and help you; I will
uphold you with my righteous right hand.
Isaiah 41:10

Seeds

———— ◊ ————

THE STRENGTH EXERTED by a seedling as it pushes its stem above the ground's surface is nothing short of amazing.... roughly 450 pounds per square inch! If God has given an organism smaller than the size of my smallest fingernail such strength, how much strength must I have inside of ME, yet untapped?

Ask yourself this question: Should my walk with God be likened to a bush or a tree? A tree stands tall against the storms of life. In times of stress it is a shelter for others. For a tree to remain upright, it must be firmly rooted in the deep earth to give it balance and support. We grow by acquiring an awareness and knowledge of God. A tree's roots often go deep enough to touch an underground stream of Living Water so that a dry spell leaves it calm and unscathed. This Living Water nourishes the tree from top to bottom. A bush, or shrub, on the other hand, only has shallow roots. These roots spread under the ground but often stay near to the surface. They seldom go downward so the bush or shrub can be easily uprooted. When there is a dry spell it cowers and withers and begins to droop and shrivel. It cannot help itself let alone help anyone else.

He who sows in <u>hope</u> will reap in <u>joy</u>! Pray for forgiveness and for knowledge as you grow deeper into a life led by the Spirit. Use this power to help you stay in the Spirit, for the harvest of the Spirit is everlasting life!

Cynthia Irish Hockins

The seed will grow well, the vine will yield its fruit,
the ground will produce its crops,
and the heavens will drop their dew. I will give
all these things as an inheritance to the remnant of this people.
Zechariah 8:12

Ruth

————— § —————

ONCE UPON A time, a man from Bethlehem in Judah took his wife and their 2 sons and journeyed to the country of Moab to live. A famine had caused wide-spread devastation and they were looking for a better place to live. This man was called Elimelech and his wife was Naomi. Their sons were Mahlon and Kilion and they were Ephrathites. We are not sure how long it was after they arrived there that Elimelech died but Naomi was then left with just her sons for a time and soon both of them married. About 10 years later we are told that both Mahlon and Kilion died. Soon after that Naomi learned that the famine had ended because the Lord had come to the aid of His people by providing food, so she decided to return to her homeland of Bethlehem and urged both daughters-in-law to return to their mothers' homes. One obeyed but the other, Ruth, refused to abandon Naomi and insisted on accompanying her to Bethlehem.

I'm sure all of us are familiar with this story because Ruth's comments to Naomi have been quoted over and over through the ages. These two women have been through a great deal up to this point in their lives. Not only did Ruth refuse to leave Naomi, but the Bible says she *clings* to Naomi and they journeyed on together.

Ruth had come to know Naomi's God and she felt her God-given place was with Naomi, no matter how difficult this journey might prove. She had grown up worshiping the gods of Moab. Like most pagan deities, these gods promised worshipers prosperity, power, and control over their own destinies. Somehow, with God's help, Ruth was able to overcome these false beliefs and she came to faith in the true and living God that Naomi worshiped. She told Naomi that Naomi's God would also be her God and she would go wherever Naomi went. Naomi realized how very determined Ruth was to go with her so she stopped urging her to leave her. Naomi was very alone at this point in her life and she needed a friend – a sister in Christ – and Ruth became that friend as she gave up the only life she had ever known to follow and care for Naomi.

Ruth and Naomi settled in Bethlehem. They were quite alone and had no one to protect or support them. Ruth volunteered to glean grain left in the fields after the harvesters had finished. It was hot, hard work – even back-breaking work – but God was also at work and help was on the way! A wealthy landowner took notice of Ruth and quietly at first, and then later more openly, he began to protect and provide for them both. Boaz came to the rescue and in time he wound up loving and marrying Ruth. Later, Ruth and Boaz were rewarded with a son, Obed, who was the father of King David. Her rewards continued long after she was gone and she is one of very few women to hold a prominent place in the genealogy of Jesus.

This story of Ruth is a beautiful lesson for each of us too. We may never know or understand why some things happen in our lives, but ultimately, God has a purpose and a reason for it all. In Him we will find the strength we need to continue. It may be weeks, months or even years before we see things coming together at times, and sometimes we may *never* fully understand our circumstances, but through prayer and with faith we can feel God's peace about whatever situations we find ourselves facing. In His service we should reach out to others unselfishly.

"Where you go I will go, and where you stay I will stay. Your people will be my people and your God my God." Ruth 1:16

Twelve

—§—

NUMBERS PLAY A very important part in many of the Books of the Bible. I feel they are always there for a reason. When something is repeated over and over, we need to pay more attention to what is being said. The number twelve is repeated often.

The twelve tribes of Israel were named for the twelve sons of Jacob. Genesis Chapter 35 lists them in the order of their birth: Reuben, Simeon, Levi, and Judah were the sons of Leah; Dan and Naphtali were the sons of Bilhah, Rachel's maidservant; Gad and Asher were the sons of Zilpah, Leah's maidservant; then Leah had two more sons, Issachar and Zebulun; and Jacob's wife Rachel was the mother of Joseph and Benjamin.

Before Jacob's time, Ishmael, son of Abraham and Sarah's handmaid, Hagar, also fathered twelve sons and twelve tribes were named for them also. In the order of their birth they were: Nebaioth, Kedar, Adbeel, Mibsam, Mishma, Dumah, Massa, Hadad, Tema, Jetur, Naphish, and Kedemah.

After crossing the Red Sea, Moses and the Israelites came to Elim and there they found twelve springs. Moses built an altar at the foot of the mountain before receiving the commandments from God in Exodus 24. This altar consisted of twelve pillars around the foot of the mountain to represent the twelve tribes.

In the book of Numbers twelve spies were sent ahead, one from each of the twelve tribes of Israel. They were sent to observe and determine the strength of the Canaanites before the children of Israel came face-to-face with them.

The book of Deuteronomy lists twelve curses which were announced at Mount Ebal. The people were told to build an altar of stones when they got to Mount Ebal. They were not to use any iron tools on these stones, and they were to offer burnt offerings on these stones when they were all in place. Then, after crossing the Jordan, six of Jacob's tribes were to stand on Mount Gerizim to bless the people and six were to stand on Mount Ebal to pronounce curses. The Levites were told to recite the curses to ALL the people of Israel in a loud voice.

In the New Testament we have the twelve disciples: Peter, Andrew, James, John, Thomas, Thaddeus, Matthew, Simon, Philip, Bartholomew, James and Judas. Later, after Jesus fed the 5000, there were twelve baskets of broken pieces left over.

In Mark, Chapter 5, we are told the story of a leader of the synagogue named Jairus who fell at Jesus' feet and begged him to heal his dying twelve year old daughter. When Jesus arrived at the home of Jairus, he was told the girl was dead, but Jesus took her by the hand and she was healed. In this same chapter, the unnamed woman who had suffered from hemorrhages for twelve years reached in to touch the cloak of Jesus in hopes of finally being healed. Jesus, sensing her touch, called her "daughter" and said that her faith had made her well and he sent her away healed of her disease. A footnote in my Bible says this is a "tender address used nowhere else in Jesus' recorded words."

Revelations, Chapter 21, makes reference to twelve angels, twelve fruits, twelve foundations, and twelve gates. Also in Revelations John said God showed him the Holy City, Jerusalem with its great, high wall with twelve gates and with twelve angels at the gates. On the gates were written the names of the twelve tribes of Israel. There were three gates on the east, three on the north, three on the south and three on the west. The wall of the city had twelve foundations, and on them were the names of the twelve apostles of the Lamb. The walls of the city were decorated with twelve different precious stones. I particularly enjoy what John says next early in Chapter 22. He said the angel showed him the river of the water of life which was bright as crystal as it flowed from the throne of God through the middle of the city. He went on to say that on either side of the river is the tree of life with its twelve kinds of fruit, producing fruit each month; and the leaves of the tree are for the healing of the nations. That paints a beautiful picture as it fills us with promises of good and wonderful things as believers. The fruits are lush and plentiful and there is healing everywhere.

Isn't it beautiful to realize how God attends to absolutely every detail? Nothing is forgotten, nothing is left out. Every miracle he performs has its own particular meaning and significance. Let's remember to give our thanks, our love and our praise regularly to our thoughtful, ever-present, loving and caring God.

If you confess with your mouth, 'Jesus is Lord,'
and believe in your heart that God raised him from the dead,
you will be saved.
Romans 10:9

Everyone who calls on the name of the Lord will be saved.
Romans 10:13

Grief

———— § ————

THE DICTIONARY DESCRIBES grief as intense emotional suffering caused by loss, disaster, etc. It also describes it as acute sorrow and deep sadness. Someone once said grief is like a hall of mirrors. Everywhere you look, you see yourself – almost as if you cannot see beyond yourself and your loss. This same person went on to say that it is not an ending. Grief is a time in your life when God offers windows. These windows open both up and out, and with time they become wider and they expand our view and broaden our horizons so we can see beyond ourselves.

Grief is also said to be a love word. That idea may surprise you, but when you take time to think about it, we do not grieve for those we do not love. After we spend some time in the low places of our grief, places hidden from everyone but God, we eventually realize that we are becoming more sensitive – more compassionate – more courageous -- more sympathetic, and more kind. All of these tender mercies help us to grow, and by reaching out to God at these times, we begin to recognize the fulfillment of God's promises. We will grieve and cry in the nighttime, but, with time, the light of day will return to our lives and we will find joy again – a joy based on God's love and God's promises. A joy that comes in the morning following our grief.

Being a child of God does not exempt us from feeling the hurt as we grieve. Jesus spoke of grieving or mourning in the Beatitudes in Matthew Chapter 5. He says those who mourn will be given courage and comfort. He does not say comfortable – he says comfort. He is there during our times of grief and pain and he will not leave us *in* that frame of mind. He will see us *THROUGH* this dark valley and bring us out on the other side.

In Psalm 23 David wrote this: *"Even though I walk through the valley of the shadow of death, I will fear no evil, for you are with me; your rod and your staff will comfort me."* David knew the rod and staff were instruments of authority that were often used to guide, prod and even rescue sheep that strayed. He was saying he knew God would watch over him and not abandon him.

Christian writer Philip Keller wrote, *"Just because I am a child of God I am NOT exempt from the downdrafts of disaster, the cross currents of calamity, or the dark, rainy, dreary days of grief and distress. These are as much a part of the warp and woof of life's tapestry as are the sun-filled days, brisk with warm sea breezes.*

"To be spiritually alive is not to be dead to hurt and pain, but to be free to experience them, trusting that God will bring us through them safely. Living through these experiences makes us different people – and difference can be good! In our period of mourning we see only sunsets. When we come OUT of mourning, we begin to see the sunrises again."

Thank God for mornings!

> *Then maidens will dance and be glad, young men and*
> *old as well. I will turn their mourning into gladness;*
> *I will give them comfort and joy instead of sorrow.*
> *Jeremiah 31:13*

The Present

———— § ————

THERE IS A present waiting for you! Today! Right now! You can take advantage of this beautiful, special gift offer by just saying "YES!" to God, either silently or out loud! This offer is free to you, and it includes the forgiveness of your sins and the guarantee of eternal life in the Kingdom of Heaven!

This offer is good right now! It was ready for you yesterday, too, but now yesterday is gone so that offer has expired. The offer <u>may</u> also be good tomorrow, providing you are still here…. but who knows what might happen between now and tomorrow? Wouldn't it be better to accept this gift now? Today? That way, you are assured that this offer has not expired – and, at least at this very moment, you are not expired either……!

To accept, please fold your hands together and either close your eyes or look up toward heaven and say these words:

Father, I want to accept You into my heart and my life right now – this very moment. I ask that You forgive my sins, come into my heart and show me Your way. Thank You for sending Your Son to die on the cross for my sins and thank You for the gift of eternal life.
Help me to be the person You want me to be!

Now, from this time forward, live in the "now." Think ahead; remember yesterday, but live in the present. Yesterday is passed and tomorrow is another day. Live in the "now" and you won't miss the joys of today! God Bless You!

Abundant Sonshine

For God so loved the world that he gave his one and only Son,
that whoever believes in him shall not perish
but have eternal life.
John 3:16

Details

---§---

RECENTLY I WAS reading in the Book of Exodus and as I read, I was reminded that God is truly a God of details. No matter is too small for our God, and He leaves nothing to chance, not only in Biblical times, but even today.

The Lord spoke to Moses in the Book of Exodus and in addition to giving Moses the well-known Ten Commandments, He also gave Moses instructions for the building of the Tabernacle as a place to honor God and to worship Him. He listed the exact size and dimensions of this tabernacle and then He went on to list details. Angels of specific sizes were to be placed in many areas and the Lord said the angel's wings were to be spread upward. These were not written instructions, as we would expect today to erect something of this size. These were oral instructions – and very lengthy ones too. Those of us who sew could compare this to creating a dress for a special occasion. We would require explicit printed instructions and we would refer to them constantly during the construction of our garment. God gave these instructions to Moses all at one time, and Moses did not have pencil and paper to take notes! He had to remember it all, and to remember it in the proper order as well.

When it came to the veil to be placed around the most holy place, the altar, the Lord listed many different types of yarns and linens of many colors. The altar itself was to be not gold, but a bronze overlay. All of the utensils were to be bronze, even the tent pegs. In the outer court He spoke of "twisted linen," bronze bases and silver hooks. He even specified that the curtains were to be made by an embroiderer.

After giving Moses the plans for the tabernacle, he went on to give Moses instructions for the clothing he and Aaron and the sons of Aaron were to wear. Their outfits were to include a breast piece. On this breast piece there were to be four rows of precious stones. These precious stones were to be: ruby, topaz, beryl, turquoise, sapphire, emerald, jacinth, agate, amethyst, chrysolite, onyx and jasper. There were 12 of them, one for each of the tribes, and they were all to be mounted in gold filigree. According to my Bible dictionary, these stones were fairly large because there were only 3 stones across and the breast piece was only 9" wide. Even the undergarments they were to wear were described in detail and they were to go from waist to thigh.

In addition to the breast piece, there was to be an ephod, a waistcoat, to be made of gold, fine twisted linen by a skilled craftsman. The robe they were to wear was to be made of blue cloth with bells and pomegranates alternated around the bottom hem. They were to wear a tunic, and a turban with an attached plate was to be on their forehead. The sash for the robe was to be made by an embroiderer. Aaron and his sons were to wear all of this and to place their hands on the head of two bulls as they were slaughtered as a sin offering. (Personally, I find it difficult to picture all of them in these beautiful, hand crafted and hand sewn outfits, standing almost on top of a bull as it was slaughtered with the blood spattered in all directions!)

After the initial slaughtering, they were to place some of this blood on their right earlobes, thumbs of the right hand and the toes of the right foot. Then the remaining blood was to be sprinkled on their garments. All of this was to be done for 7 days. This rich symbolism emphasizes the Deity of the Lord and also to what degree He wanted to be respected. It stresses the important role that worshiping Him is to take.

Although some of these instructions may have seemed strange – or even impossible – to Moses, Aaron and the sons of Aaron, because they were all men of God they did not question God. They followed His instructions to the letter!

Another example of God being a God of details was demonstrated in our creation as human beings. Absolutely every detail was thought of even before we were born – bone, tissue, muscle, skin color, cartilage, eye color and eyelids, finger and toenails, teeth and tongues – even the soles of our feet and our earlobes were all planned out and each was created for a specific function. Genesis 1:26 & 27 tell us that God created man on the sixth day. Think of that! As intricate and complex as the human body is, He did it all in one day – on the sixth day of creation – and you may recall that sixth day followed five very busy days!

We are SO blessed and SO fortunate! Our God is a God of love! He is also a God of compassion! A God who nurtures and understands us because of, and sometimes even in spite of, our individual idiosyncrasies and our natural tendencies toward procrastination. In expressing our thanks to Him in our daily prayers, let's add a new thought. Let's remember to thank Him for planning all of the details of us and of our lives!

Are not five sparrows sold for two pennies?
Yet not one of them is forgotten by God.
Indeed, the very hairs of your head are all numbered.
Don't be afraid; you are worth more than many sparrows.
Luke 12:6-7

Happy

Good morning, Jesus,

I have noticed that the faces around a "happy face" often seem to reflect that happiness. Starting this morning, if my face is a happy one, and my heart is glad, maybe it will rub off onto my family, and when they leave and go about their day, their faces can start a <u>new</u> circle of happy faces and hearts. Let others I encounter see your love in my happy face, Lord, and let them want to be part of this growing, happy circle, today and every day.

A happy face means a glad heart.
Proverbs 5:13

Happy is he who has the God of Jacob for his help,
whose hope is in the Lord his God.
Psalm 146:5

Worry

———— § ————

In Gracia Burnham's book "To Fly Again" she wrote about the futility of worry. She spoke of all the things she and her husband Martin had to worry about while they were in captivity in the Philippines. They were missionaries who were kidnapped by an Al Qaida group and held hostage for over a year in the jungles. When they were finally rescued Martin was shot and he died before they reached freedom. During their ordeal she had a lot of time to think and reflect and she credits Martin's strong faith with helping her overcome their daily difficulties. His strength lifted her up constantly while they were captives.

The dictionary defines worry as "To torment oneself with disturbing thoughts." To worry is to be anxious or to be in a troubled state of mind. It is a form of anxiety. I think it is interesting to note that one of the next words in the dictionary is "worse" – and then comes "worsen." When we worry, the situation becomes even worse! But the most important thing to notice here is that we bring this on ourselves! We initiate the worry. We choose to worry – and if we can choose to worry, then we can also choose not to worry! The root word for worry traces back to the Old English word "wyrgan" which means to strangle. That is precisely what worry does to us – it cuts off our air! It prevents us from inhaling and drawing in the Holy Spirit. If we let it, it will slowly asphyxiate us!

When worry controls us, it is like we are saying God cannot be trusted with this particular problem. We're demonstrating a lack of faith! We are implying He does not care so He probably won't do anything about it anyway so we'll have to do all this worrying on our own. We'll just have to keep on worrying through this entire situation. We experience frustration and we become more and more frazzled. But if we turn to our faith, and turn to God, those thoughts will be changed. We will soon realize that God <u>does</u> care! By working together, He and I can change my attitude if I just let Him. We should be grateful that we don't know what's ahead for us because that's actually less to worry about! My current situation itself may not change, but my approach to it and how I deal with it will be changed. If I'll just supply the willingness to listen and remember to rely on Him, He will supply the power – and together, He and I can accomplish anything!

Let's go back to the dictionary for a moment. The word right after worsen is a powerful one! Worship! That word is described as an intense love – a deep admiration – a religious reverence – a feeling or offering of great devotion and respect. The verse below is a perfect antidote for worrying.

> *"Don't worry about anything; instead, pray about everything.*
> *Tell God what you need, and thank Him for*
> *all he has done. When you do this,*
> *you will experience God's wonderful peace."*
> *Philippians 4:6-7*

Wet Cement

———— ◊ ————

Lord,

I passed a sign today that said "WET CEMENT." It was attached to a cord roping off a portion of newly-poured sidewalk. In one corner I saw a shoe print, and in another corner a set of handprints and initials and a crudely drawn smiling face. I shook my head as I walked around it wondering who would do such a thing. Surely these people knew better!

Then, Father, I thought of some of the absolutely dumb things I find myself doing at times. Like giving in to sin and temptation when I really know better! Lots of them have warning signs on them telling me to stay clear, but I don't always heed those warnings. Sometimes I plunge ahead and "leave my initials."

Help me to remember, Lord, that I don't have to leave my "mark."
If I can just remember to ask for help, You
will come to my rescue and steer me
away from temptations. YOU are my
strength, Father, and I thank You!

I press on toward the goal to win the prize for which God
has called me heavenward in Christ Jesus.
Philippians 3:14

Needs Versus Wants

———— § ————

ONE CHAPTER IN the book of Mark in the Bible tells the story of two very different men and how they each sought an audience with Jesus as he traveled through Judea. Each of these men pushed their way through large crowds in an effort to get nearer to Jesus. Jesus responded to each of them by asking what each wanted. Actually, he already knew what each man wanted but it was his intent to have them express their needs out loud.

The rich young ruler called him "Good Teacher." He asked Jesus how he could attain the gift of eternal life he'd heard so much about. When Jesus told him it would be necessary to give up all his wealth, riches and worldly goods, he refused and turned away sadly.

The other man, Bartimaeus, called him "Jesus, Son of David." He was a beggar and his only possession was the cloak on his back. When Jesus agreed to talk to him he cast even that meager cloak aside and hurried to Him and asked for his sight that he might see Jesus in person.

The rich young ruler kept his wealth and lost eternal life. Bartimaeus received more than just his sight because of his faith. He may have lost his thread-bare cloak but he did see Jesus and he gained the gift of heaven!

When we are tempted by worldly possessions and blinded by the "things" of this world, it would help us to think of these two men in the Bible. Let's remember the example of Bartimaeus and "cast off our cloak" as we follow Jesus.

Then Jesus said to his disciples, "If anyone would come after me
he must deny himself and take up his cross and follow me.
For whoever wants to save his life will lose it, but whoever loses his life
for me will find it. What good will it be for
a man if he gains the whole world,
yet forfeits his soul? Or what can a man give in exchange for his soul?
For the Son of Man is going to come in his Father's glory
with his angels, and then he will reward each per-
son according to what he has done.
Matthew 16:24-27

Fear

---§---

THE DICTIONARY DEFINES fear as anxiety caused by danger, evil, pain or fright. It is a feeling of uneasiness or apprehension. My Bible Concordance describes it as "anxiety caused by approaching danger."

In one Old Testament example, Jacob expressed great fear when he wanted to return to his homeland to face his brother Esau whom he had betrayed when he stole Esau's birthright many years earlier. He wanted to make amends, but he was afraid because he did not know what kind of reception he might receive. He put himself into God's hands and Esau welcomed him with open arms and a forgiving heart.

Later, in the New Testament, immediately following the death of Jesus on the cross, the Centurion and those with him who were guarding Jesus experienced an earthquake and were fearful and very afraid. Matthew 27 tells us how the curtain of the Temple was torn, top to bottom, and the earth shook and tombs broke open. No wonder they were afraid and feared for their safety! Matthew says the Centurion was terrified and said, "Surely he was the Son of God."

My Bible Concordance lists well over 200 verses that speak of Godly fear or reverential awe. In addition to that list, the human examples given include Noah, Abraham, Jacob, Joseph, David, Obadiah, Job and Nehemiah. These are all men of the Old Testament. It is interesting that the next word in the Concordance is "fearlessness," meaning to be without fear, and several of the men I just listed also appear here along with Peter, John and Paul from the New Testament.

Now, let's think about being fear<u>less</u> and talk about fear <u>not</u> and do <u>not</u> fear. It's been said there are about 80 "fear nots" in the Bible and I don't know how many "do not fears" we might find. Psalm 27, first verse, says *"The Lord is my light and my salvation – whom shall I fear?"* In Psalm 56 David wrote this: *"When I am afraid, I will trust in you. In God I trust; I will not be afraid. What can mortal man do to me?"* There are a couple verses in Isaiah 41 that remind us not to fear. In verse 10 it says, *"So do not fear, for I am with you; do not be dismayed for I am your God. I will strengthen you and help you; I will uphold you with my righteous right hand."* A bit later, in verse 13 it says, *"For I am the Lord, your God, who takes hold of your right hand and says to you, Do not fear; I will help you."* God just cannot say it any more clearly than that! He is with us; He will help us; He will uphold us; and He will take hold of our right hand. What beautiful images those words express. Let these promises fill your heart and mind!

The opposite of fear is trust, and the Psalms are filled with examples and advantages of trust over fear. Psalm 33:21 says, *"In him our hearts rejoice for we trust in his holy name."* My Bible concordance lists many benefits of trusting and these include joy, triumph, safety and guidance. God says He will guide us and guard us if we but trust in him and "fear not." Let these promises fill your heart and mind! Be fearless!

> *There is no fear in love. Perfect love drives*
> *out fear because fear has to do with*
> *punishment. The one who fears is not made per-*
> *fect in love.   I John 4:18*
> *I sought the Lord and he heard me and deliv-*
> *ered me from all my fears.   Psalm 34:4*

Hospitality

THE DICTIONARY SAYS that hospitality is the act or practice or quality of being hospitable. I didn't feel that explained it very well so I looked up hospitable. To be hospitable is to show kindness, friendliness and solicitude toward guests. It also says it means to be open and receptive to new ideas. One of the places in the Bible that speaks of hospitality is in the 12th chapter of Romans. However, hospitality in some form or other is referenced in 11 books of the Bible and in at least 7 books, examples are given.

In verse 8 in the Romans chapter, we are told to encourage others, to contribute to their needs and to give generously; and it also says that in leadership we should govern diligently, and in showing mercy we are to do it cheerfully. Paul is referring to our spiritual gifts here when he describes how we should act and behave and live our lives in a Christian manor. He talks about loving and how we should regard evil and be patient in our tribulations or trials as well as our personal life.

Verses 9 to 21 are filled with demonstrations of different types and examples of hospitality. My NIV Bible heads this group of verses with the title of "Love." Paul begins here by saying love, or hospitality, must be sincere. He goes on to say we are to be devoted to one another in brotherly love, and we must honor one another above ourselves.

Stop a minute and think about some of your friends. We very often enjoy different people for different reasons. Some friends may enjoy eating lunch or dinner in a favorite restaurant once in a while – others may like to shop or browse through a shopping center – or perhaps they like to play cards or table games – Another may like to walk and visit for exercise, or just share a pot of coffee or tea and visit. Each of these friends are different in their own ways, and yet they all fall into the category of friends.

Hospitality works that way too. You can be hospitable by inviting people to your home for a meal together – or by taking a prepared meal or treats to a shut-in or a family going through a crisis of some kind. You show hospitality in the way you treat your guests and in what you do to make their visit more comfortable. If you are warm and cordial and welcoming, these friends will want to return.

We should each be practicing hospitality every day in all of our dealings with others. It should not matter if it is a waiter or busboy, or a store clerk, or a receptionist in an office situation – each deserves to be treated with an air of cordiality and hospitality – meaning we are to be polite and pleasant. One of my husband's favorite expressions was "kill them with kindness." He often said that to our kids when they complained about a teacher or classmate or playmate -- and it must have made an impression because I have heard my daughter say that same thing to her children! And she's also told me about several instances where she herself has practiced it, often with good results! We all know that often this is easier said than done, but keep trying. Go ahead – and "kill them with kindness!"

"If your enemy is hungry, feed him; if he is
thirsty, give him something to drink.
In doing this, you will heap burning coals on his head.
Do not be overcome by evil, but overcome evil with good."
Romans 12:21

Share with God's people who are in need.
Practice hospitality. Romans 12:13b

ABC's of Positive Thinking

———— ◊ ————

Uplifting verses to enlighten and encourage.

A	Romans 8:28	<u>All</u> things work for the good of those who love him.
B	John 20:31	<u>Believe</u> that Jesus is the Son of God that you may have life.
C	Joshua 24:15	<u>Choose</u> this day whom you will serve.
D	Romans 12:17	<u>Do</u> not repay anyone evil for evil.
E	Philippians 2:4	<u>Each</u> of you should look not only to your own interests, but also to the interests of others.
F	I Timothy 6:12	<u>Fight</u> the good fight of the faith; lay hold on eternal life.
G	Philippians 1:2	<u>Grace</u> and peace to you from God our Father and the Lord Jesus Christ.
H	Proverbs 15:13	<u>Happy</u> hearts make faces cheerful.
I	Proverbs 3:6	<u>In</u> all your ways acknowledge Him and He will direct your paths.
J	Luke 6:37	<u>Judge</u> not, and you shall not be judged.
K	I Timothy 5:22	<u>Keep</u> yourself pure.
L	I Corinthians 13:8	<u>Love</u> never fails.
M	James 2:13	<u>Mercy</u> triumphs over judgment!
N	Luke 16:13	<u>No</u> servant can serve two masters.

O	Exodus 12:24	<u>Obey</u> these instructions as a lasting ordinance for you and your descendants.
P	Ephesians 6:23	<u>Peace</u> to the brothers, and love and faith from God the Father and the Lord Jesus Christ.
Q	Ecclesiastes 9:17	<u>Quiet</u> words of the wise should be heard rather than the shout of a ruler of fools.
R	Philippians 4:4	<u>Rejoice</u> in the Lord always. I will say it again: Rejoice!
S	Ephesians 5:21	<u>Submit</u> to one another out of reverence for Christ.
T	Mark 1:11	<u>Then</u> a voice came from heaven, "You are My beloved Son, in whom I am well pleased."
U	Ephesians 5:17	<u>Understand</u> what the Lord's will is and do not be foolish.
V	Mark 15:38	<u>Verily</u> I say to you, he rejoices more over that (found) sheep than of the ninety-nine that never went astray.
W	Deuteronomy 5:33	<u>Walk</u> in the ways which the Lord your God has commanded…
X	II Corinthians 13:5	<u>(e)Xamine</u> yourselves often to see whether you are still in the faith.
Y	I Corinthians 6:20	<u>You</u> are not your own; you were bought with a price.
Z	Isaiah 1:27	<u>Zion</u> will be redeemed with justice, and her penitent ones with righteousness.

Rest

————— § —————

THE DICTIONARY SAYS rest means peace. It means refreshing inactivity, or a relief from anything that is distressing, either mentally or physically – and we could probably even say emotionally. Rest is an absence of motion. The dictionary also says that to renew is to revive. We can be refreshed, renewed and revived occasionally by ceasing work of any kind and by resting, even if it is just for a little while. The dictionary also says that to refresh is also to replenish. We can do our bodies and our minds a great service by allowing them to rest now and then – to be completely free from everything that surrounds us. In fact, we will often find our minds and bodies function better following a rest or change in our normal routines.

Too often we think of resting as wasting our time. We think we have to keep busy and keep forging ahead and we must keep on doing things to justify our existence. On the contrary! We NEED rest in order to restore ourselves and renew our bodies AND our minds. Jesus knew the need for and the value of rest, and He also knew the positive results that would come from it.

In the very beginning of the Bible, early in the 2nd chapter of Genesis, it says, *"By the seventh day God had finished the work He had been doing; so on the seventh day He rested from all His work. And God blessed the seventh day and made it holy, because on it He rested from all the work of creating that He had done."*

In Isaiah God tells us *"In repentance and rest is your salvation, in quietness and trust is your strength..."* In Mark, before the crowds gathered for the feeding of the 5000, the apostles had gathered around Jesus to report to Him all they had done and taught. Jesus replied telling them to come with Him to a quiet place to get some rest. Eventually they were recognized and followed and the crowds gathered to listen to Jesus, but Jesus and the disciples had fortified themselves for this with a few moments of rest. They were all renewed, refreshed, and ready to go on.

Jesus, too, knew the value of rest for himself. He often felt the need to set himself apart from the crowds and the disciples, to be alone with His Father, because this type of rest was also a renewal for Him. He used this time to talk and pray to His Father, the Almighty God. Afterward He always felt uplifted and energized because He had taken this time to rest. Jesus also made reference to rest for the weary in Matthew Chapter 11 when He said, *"Come to me, all you who are weary and burdened, and I will give you rest. Take my yoke upon you and learn from me, for I am gentle and humble in heart, and you will find rest for your souls."* He then added, *"For my yoke is easy and my burden is light."* What we need to remember here is that by yoking two animals together in one harness, the two share the workload. They automatically work together and neither one of them is over-burdened because the load is shared equally. In this passage of the Bible, Jesus is telling us to yoke ourselves to Him and our burdens will be lessened immediately because of His reassuring presence. I'm sure each of us can think of many times over the years when we turned a problem or situation over to Him and immediately we felt the burden fall from our shoulders because the problem was now shared with the One who is in charge.

Another verse from Isaiah comes to mind here. Chapter 40, verse 31 says, *"But those who hope in the Lord will renew their strength. They will soar on wings like eagles, they will run and not grow weary, they will walk and not be faint."* Isaiah is stressing the goodness of God and he reminds us such a God is able to deliver and restore His people if they will wait in faith for Him to act. They are to trust in Him and to draw strength from Him and from His presence. When we do this <u>we</u> are renewed – refreshed – and replenished, and we are also ready for whatever comes our way.

In Psalm 55 David spoke of rest because he was being pursued and threatened by a former friend. David felt there was danger in every direction for him and he said, *"Oh, that I had the wings of a dove! I would fly away and be at rest…. I would be in my place of shelter, far from the tempest and the storm."* He knew the value and importance of setting himself "apart," and he also knew the importance of turning to God when he felt overburdened.

To be refreshed is to be renewed or restored. In Acts 3:19 Peter spoke to a group after the healing of a crippled beggar. He challenged those who were listening to repent and to turn to God so their sins might be wiped out and that would be a time of refreshing and renewal, the kind that can only come from God Himself.

So let's remember. We need to rest to be refreshed, to be restored, to be renewed, to be replenished, to be rejuvenated, so we are ready to serve whenever and wherever God calls on us. But don't rest on your laurels – rest in the Lord!

Be still before the Lord and wait patiently for him….. and remember, He cannot communicate with us if we don't take the time to listen when He tries to get our attention.

> *"Repent, then, and turn to God,*
> *so that your sins may be wiped out,*
> *that times of refreshing may come from the Lord,*
> *and that he may send the Christ, who has been appointed*
> *for you – even Jesus."*
> *Acts 3:19, 20*

> *"For Moses said, 'The Lord your God will raise up for you*
> *a prophet like me from among your own people;*
> *you must listen to everything he tells you.'"*
> *Acts 3:22*

Weeds

———— § ————

ONCE IN A while when I was young my mother asked me to help in our family vegetable and flower gardens. My brother and I would take turns as we watered it all faithfully and tried to keep the weeds pulled. One time my mom discovered I had missed some weeds in a section and she called me over to where she was standing.

"I'll bet you thought these were flowers, didn't you?" she asked with a smile.

"But they <u>are</u> flowers, Mom," I said defensively. "Look – these leaves are just like those next to it – the leaves with the buds on them!"

"Look again!" said Mom. "They seem to be alike, but when you take a closer look you can see they are slightly different. If we don't pull this weed out, it will choke off the real plant next to it! Also, we must take it out very carefully to be sure we get the whole root and yet not hurt the 'real' plant growing nearby."

When I looked closer, I could see some differences and I went back over the rest of my row and found several others that had fooled me. Out they came!

"Weeds in our garden are a lot like sin in our lives," Mom said as we worked together. "Many sins try to disguise themselves and if we are not careful to weed them out, root and all, they will work their way permanently into our lives and they will choke out Jesus! Many times it might seem very innocent, but any one sin can lead to SO many others!"

Now that I am grown, I think of that whenever I see people tending their gardens. They are taking care of their plants and flowers and at the same time, they are reminding us to look carefully at our lives to be sure we are weeding out any potential sins, so we can allow Christ to help us "bloom forth."

The Lord will surely comfort Zion
and will look with compassion on all her ruins;
he will make her deserts like Eden,
her wastelands like the garden of the Lord.
Isaiah 51:3

Oasis

————— ◊ —————

CLOSE YOUR EYES for just a minute. What is the first thing you think of when you hear the word oasis? What sort of scene does that word conjure up in your mind? Endless sand? Terrible thirst? Steamy sun? I immediately think of water – and I think of shade from a tree with thick leaves and branches offering shady relief from that hot, burning sun. I can picture low tree branches wafting in the breeze and I can almost hear the rustle of the water lapping up onto the sand. (I also see a padded lounge chair under that tree and a good book nearby – but that's another story!)

An oasis means relief – it is a place of respite and refreshment for body and soul. But think! That's what God promises us! He beckons to us and welcomes us with the offer of Himself as our Water of Life – the Living Water we need to sustain us and to help us refocus in any time of difficulty, whether it's during an illness or a sorrow of some kind. He told the Samaritan woman at the well that those who drink the Living Water from His well will never thirst. They will be sated and satisfied – they will be refreshed and renewed. They will be restored and ready to refocus and move forward. They will have no fear because they will have satisfied their bodily need for water by saturating their body and their soul with His life-giving Water.

The word oasis does not appear in the Bible. The dictionary says an oasis is a fertile place in a desert, due to the presence of water. It is also described as any place or thing that offers welcome relief in the midst of difficulty. When we need an oasis of some kind to carry us over or through a situation, the words of God and Jesus in the Bible have beautiful promise after promise of what we can expect and enjoy when we take the Lord into our hearts and surrender our lives – and our concerns – to Him.

> *"If anyone is thirsty, let him come to me and*
> *drink. Whoever believes in me, as*
> *the Scripture has said, streams of living wa-*
> *ter will flow from within him.*
> *John 7:37, 38*

> *The Lord said, "I have loved you with a love that never gives up.*
> *I have led you with love and kindness.*
> *Jeremiah 31:3*

> *Cast all your anxieties on Him, for He cares about you.*
> *I Peter 5:7*

> *And this is the confidence which we have*
> *in Him, that if we ask anything*
> *according to His will, He hears us.*
> *I John 5:14*

> *The words of the Lord are true. Everything God says*
> *and does can be utterly relied upon.*
> *Psalm 33:4*

Fisherman

———— § ————

THE MOST FAMOUS fisherman in the Bible was Simon Peter. He later became known as Peter, or "The Rock." No other Peter is mentioned in the Bible. He was the son of Jonas and the brother of Andrew. The Sea of Galilee figured prominently in the life of Peter several times. It was there that he was called by Jesus as he was preparing to go fishing. Later, he attempted to walk on the water of this sea to reach Jesus, and it was at the Sea of Galilee that Peter and other disciples saw and ate with Jesus following His Resurrection.

Peter had what might be called both a "positive" and a "negative" personality. He was never afraid to voice an opinion; he was courageous and bold but he also cowardly; he was often the spokesman for the other disciples (by his OWN choice and not theirs); he was a witness to the raising of Jabirus' daughter and to the Transfiguration; he was the first disciple to acknowledge Jesus as the son of God; he was with Jesus when he was arrested in the garden of Gethsemane; he denied knowing Jesus 3 times following his arrest; and he was the first to enter the tomb after Jesus' resurrection.

We can take great comfort in the story of the life of Peter. He followed Jesus and although he wavered and even denied Him, Jesus welcomed him back into His fold and He helped him become stronger, bolder and more courageous as Peter helped spread the Words of Christianity to Jews and Gentiles alike.

As Jesus was walking beside the Sea of Galilee, he saw
two brothers, Simon called Peter and his brother
Andrew. They were casting a net into the lake, for they were
fishermen. "Come, follow me," Jesus said, "and I will make you
fishers of men." At once they left their nets and followed him.
Matthew 4:18-20

Anger

ANGER IS AN emotion, one created by God. Anger is not a sin unless it becomes uncontrolled anger and it can then lead us to sin. Anger and temper are two emotions that must be <u>con</u>fessed and <u>ex</u>pressed but not <u>sup</u>pressed. If we lose our temper in a display of anger, it is often because we are out of control and the result will be that we will be less than God intends us to be. Temper, the ability to get angry, is a God-given capacity for each of us. Technically, we can never actually "lose" our temper – but we must learn to control it by looking behind our anger to recognize its cause. Try looking into a mirror when you are angry!

In the Bible, Cain is the first example of uncontrolled anger because in anger he slew his brother Abel. Afterward, God was not angry with Cain. Instead, He offered him an opportunity to confess and repent, but Cain chose not to do so. Anger doesn't surface quickly. Often it takes root and it grows. This is the kind of anger that controlled Cain, and he paid the price.

There are many incidences of anger mentioned throughout the Bible, the right kind and the wrong kind. The Lord became angry with Moses when Moses felt too inadequate to do what the Lord had commanded of him. Moses was angry when he broke the stone tablets because the people were worshiping golden idols. The Lord was also angry with Solomon because Solomon's heart had turned away from the Lord. Nehemiah became angry at the leaders who exploited the common people. In this case it was a form of social injustice that led to his anger. In the New Testament, Jesus was angry with a righteous anger when he cleared the Temple of the moneychangers because that was not the intended use of the Temple.

Florence Nightingale was a lantern-carrying, white-robed angel of mercy, but she was also a white-hot, stubborn, high-tempered woman who heard the call of God, and in her righteous anger she bullied and fought for decent treatment of the sick and wounded everywhere. Abraham Lincoln once watched a female slave being torn from her family as she was sold and he became angry. We all know about the changes resulting from his righteous anger. English prisons were vermin-infested hellholes until a man named John Howard got angry and helped bring about changes. He felt even those who had broken the law were entitled to decent treatment.

In the 1930's a pair of nurses opened a birth control clinic in Milwaukee, Wisconsin, and taught sex education classes to adults despite tremendous opposition. My fraternal grandmother, Lucina Irish Brown, was proud to be their secretary, and she went on to publish an educational booklet on sex education for young people in 1934. These women were angry that women's rights were being violated by their lack of knowledge and education, and they fought to change that – and they did! This was another form of righteous anger.

Proverbs says a fool gives full vent to his anger, but a wise man keeps himself under control. In Ephesians Paul said, "In your anger, do not sin; do not let the sun go down while you are still angry." Let's try letting God direct and channel our anger so we use it for Him.

An angry man stirs up dissension, and a hot-tempered one
commits many sins.
Proverbs 29:22

Pray

Lord,

I just read some of Your Words in I Thessalonians where You challenge us to pray constantly and to give thanks in all circumstances because this is Your will for us. The praying part isn't hard, Lord. I love praying and talking and sharing with You. And the thanking part – that isn't too difficult either, as I have SO much for which to be thankful. It's nice to say thanks for all the blessings and the good things in my life. But the bad things, too, Lord? You want me to pray for them and then to even <u>thank</u> You for them? That's hard! It's not easy to thank You for things I don't want in my life – things that hurt, either physically or emotionally.

Now I found some more of Your Words, Father. This time they are in I Peter 1:6 where You say, "For a little while you may have to suffer various trials, so that the genuineness of your faith may grow..." That helps, Father. When I can know that some good is apt to come out of the bad, that makes it a little easier to say thanks to You.

Thank You when You help me grow in my faith. Thank You when You make me stronger because I am acknowledging a weakness. Thank You for caring – for patience – and most of all, thank You that I am important to You! Even me! Thank You for being there at every turn, both the bad ones and the good ones!

Be joyful always; pray continually; give thanks in all circumstances,
for this is God's will for you in Christ Jesus.
I Thessalonians 5:16-18

Service

———— § ————

WHAT DO YOU think of when you hear the word "service?" Although it can be a noun or an adjective, it can also be a transitive verb which means it takes a direct object to complete its meaning. This would imply an action, and that's the kind of service we are talking about here. The dictionary says service is work done or a duty performed for others. It says service is functioning, helpful, and useful. Would this describe you?

Service is a duty. It is a responsibility, and it is often a challenge. But, above all, it is a privilege when the service is directed to our Lord. Remember this, too – a serving heart is one that is <u>available</u>! A serving heart is also one that is <u>grateful</u>! Psalm 100:2 says we are to serve the Lord with gladness. A serving heart is also <u>faithful</u>! I Peter 4:10-11 says this: *"Each one should use whatever gift he has received to serve others, faithfully administering God's grace in its various forms. If anyone speaks, he should do it as one speaking the very words of God. If anyone serves, he should do it with the strength God provides, so that in all things God may be praised through Jesus Christ."* We should also remember that we honor God by starting and finishing tasks He gives to us.

Jesus gave many examples of service in His ministry. He served God, His Father, when He cleared the temple of the moneychangers in Matthew 21:13, because he said, *"It is written, My house shall be a house of prayer."* He served by healing Jew and Gentile alike. He served by washing the feet of His disciples. He followed this service-action with the admonition, *"I have set an example that you should do as I have done."* But his greatest demonstration of service was His long walk to the cross and His death there so that we might have eternal life with Him.

Here are some other Bible verses dealing with service:

1. John 12:26 refers to serving and following Jesus, but above all, it stresses *"where I am my servant also will be."* It says, *"Whoever serves me must follow me, and where I am, my servant also will be. My Father will honor the one who serves me."*
2. Romans 14:18 says, *"...because anyone who serves Christ in this way is pleasing to God and approved by men."*
3. Colossians 3:22 challenges us to be sincere of heart and God-fearing, and we are further reminded to do everything as to the Lord and not to men. It says, *"Slaves, obey your earthly masters in everything; and do it, not only when their eye is on you and to win their favor, but with sincerity of heart and reverence for the Lord."*
4. Deuteronomy 11:1 says, *"Love the Lord your God and keep his requirements, his decrees, his laws and his commands always."*
5. Deuteronomy 11:13-14a says, *"So if you faithfully obey the commands I am giving you today, to love the Lord your God and serve him with all your heart and with all your soul, then I will send rain on your land in its season."* (This same phrase is repeated in John 22:5 and also in I Samuel 12:20.)

In his coronation speech in 1937, King George VI said, "The highest distinction is service to others." His kind of service would be different from what God expects of us, but in the eyes of the Lord, it is all the same. He says, *"I tell you the truth, whatever you did for one of the least of these brothers of mine, you did for me,"* (Matthew 25:40) and he concludes this portion of scripture with the promise *"the righteous will go away to eternal life."* That is His promise! That is our goal!

In Galatians 5:13 there is another reference to serving and this one challenges us to serve one another in love. Elsewhere we are told to be "fervent in spirit" and "given to hospitality." Hospitality is a form of service and it is also a gift! When it is used correctly, it does not impress, it serves. Think about the innkeeper in Bethlehem. He served the Lord. He had no rooms in his inn but he offered what he had. The stable offered no comforts, but it did offer room, and that was what was needed at that moment! The innkeeper did not realize it, but he was using his gift of hospitality and his gift of serving!

No task, no service, if done to the glory of God, is too small. We cannot all serve in the same ways, but each of us can do something that will benefit someone, and in so doing, we please and serve the Lord! Some serve by preaching or teaching, some by cooking or cleaning, some by singing solos and others by adding to a chorus. Above all, whatever you do, do it with a sincere heart and with a joy and a dedication to God.

Try this experiment: take a pencil and paper and make a list of several talents you have that could be used to serve the Lord. It may be something as simple as baking cookies for a neighbor who's having difficulty of some kind, whether it's personal, physical, or emotional. A friend or neighbor might appreciate knowing you are going to the grocery store or the drugstore so you could pick up items for them. Perhaps you could occasionally play the piano at a local nursing home. I know most nursing homes have pianos and the staff and residents always welcome someone who will sit down and play any kind of music. You might offer to clean cupboards in the church kitchen – or read to a shut-in or someone with vision problems – or offer to help write a note for them to a friend or relative. None of these things would take a lot of time, but each will bring joy to many. Some tasks are more demanding than others, but they all have an inner reward when they are done with joy and to the glory of God.

Search me, O God, and know my heart; test
me and know my anxious thoughts.
Psalm 148:23

Faith is . . .

. . . a gift from God, freely given, to all who ask.

. . . what you believe about the person of Jesus Christ.

. . . a spontaneous outgoing of my person to another whom I know.

. . . a choice that can be weakened and even destroyed by doubt.

. . . increased by exercise and usage.

. . . something that grows with self-surrender.

. . . not seen, but the results of faith can be seen in a person's life.

. . . the bird who sings while it is still dark.

. . . the crocus that pushes its way upward through the snow.

SOMEONE ONCE SAID that a little faith will bring your soul to heaven, but a lot of faith will bring heaven to your soul. Another said faith can be summed up with five action verbs: to fear, to walk, to love, to serve, and to keep. Each of these words is used often in the Bible, and each is closely related to the others. Reverence toward God and love for God are actions that stimulate other actions. Companionship with God, obedience to God, and service for God are possible through the actions of reverence and love.

In order to flourish, inward faith must be outwardly obvious.

Self-Esteem

---
§

SELF-ESTEEM IS SAID to be one of the keys to happiness, contentment and peace of mind. In many ways, it is also a mental condition. If we want to feel good about ourselves, we must feel good about our surroundings and our world as well as who we associate with and what we accomplish.

We gain self-esteem by becoming competent – by acquiring a sense of feeling capable. When we are satisfied with ourselves, with our ability to live and to function, we feel better and more confident and this increases our inner self-esteem. By doing this, we must not allow ourselves to be caught in a web of comparing ourselves to others. Each of us is an individual. Each of us is a one-of-a-kind. No one else has the same fingerprints or the same voice or the same personality that you have. No one has the exact same genes and chromosomes either. Since the beginning of time, there has never been another person exactly like you, and until the end of all creation, there never will be another you! To put it simply, each of us is unique. The very hairs on our heads are numbered and God knows every unique characteristic we each possess. Because each of us is unique, we cannot be compared. Always remember, life is not a competition. God accepts us, God values us, and God evaluates us according to what we do with what we have been given.

We get self-esteem by fully accepting God's grace and what it really means to us individually. God's grace means that He forgives us unconditionally for our limitations and our sins, both deliberate and accidental, when we approach Him in a spirit of sincerity and in an attitude of repentance.

Self-esteem is somewhat based on knowledge. Book knowledge may give a person many college degrees and allow for achievement, accomplishment and even public recognition, but without wisdom, that knowledge could easily be used for evil. Knowledge invents a knife or a gun, but wisdom uses it.

Count yourself lucky! Think positively about yourself! Sit up a little straighter! Stand a little taller! Smile more and the energy and self-esteem you feel will then be evident to others – and then they will sit up a little straighter and perhaps they will smile more too!

> *Though the Lord is on high, he looks upon the lowly,*
> *but the proud he knows from afar. Though*
> *I walk in the midst of trouble,*
> *you preserve my life; you stretch out your*
> *hand against the anger of my foes,*
> *with your right hand you save me. The Lord*
> *will fulfill his purpose for me;*
> *your love, O Lord, endures forever – do not aban-*
> *don the works of your hands.*
> *Psalm 138:7, 8*

Wind

——— § ———

WE HEAR A lot about the wind, especially when we listen to weather forecasters. They talk about tropical winds heading toward land and dissipating over waters and they caution us about severe winds that may break into sudden storms, tornados or hurricanes that can cause anything from minor inconveniences to sheer, utter devastation. These forecasters often give us updates on the direction of the wind and the speed of the wind, and it is part of their responsibility to caution us about severe winds and potential storms.

Yes, we can feel the wind, especially when it messes up a new hair-do, or it blows our clothes around, or reverses our umbrellas. Although we may feel it, in reality we cannot actually see the wind. What we see are the results of the wind. Sometimes you can feel it as a soft breeze or a welcome stirring when it's especially hot, and other times it might feel like a strong gale, but regardless of how you feel it, it tells you a lot about what is going on around you. It can cause branches to dip and sway here and there, but it can also topple trees and even buildings -- and it can move a person, a car, a truck or a train in a direction other than where it is planning to go. It can force us to change our direction because we simply don't have the strength to fight it. You may try to fight the wind, but in the end, it's a lot easier to let it take you where it wants to go or find a place of refuge.

The Bible has quite a bit to say about winds and their directions. It speaks of 8 miracles associated with the wind. Seven were in the Old Testament and the only one in the New Testament is described in Matthew 8 during a storm. Jesus was sleeping and his frightened disciples woke him. Matthew 8:26 says

Jesus responded with*: "O, you of little faith, why are you so afraid?" and he rebuked the wind.* In Proverbs 25:23 it says, *"As a <u>north</u> wind brings rain, so a sly tongue brings angry looks."* In Jeremiah 18:17 it says, *"Like a wind from the <u>east</u>, I will scatter them before their enemies; I will show them my back and my face in the day of their disaster."* In Acts 27:13-15 Paul says, *"When a gentle <u>south</u> wind began to blow, they thought they had obtained what they wanted, so they weighed anchor and sailed along the shore of Crete. Before long, a wind of hurricane force, called the 'northeaster,' swept down from the island. The ship was caught by the storm and could not head into the wind; so we gave way to it and were driven along."* In the book of Ezekiel, in Chapter 37, Ezekiel is speaking of God and he says, *"Then he said to me, 'Prophesy to the breath; prophesy, son of man, and say to it, "This is what the Sovereign Lord says: Come from the <u>four</u> <u>winds</u>, O breath, and breathe into these slain that they may live. So I prophesied as he commanded me, and breath entered them; they came to life and stood up on their feet – a vast army."*

In many ways you could say winds are like God. We cannot see Him, but we know He is there. We can feel or sense His presence as we go about our daily lives. If we will only allow Him, He will gladly bring His calmness into our busy schedules. There are some who deny Him and His presence. They ignore Him, but He's still there. They haven't yet realized that going against His teachings can be a bit like fighting the wind as you walk into it. Remember this when life becomes a bit overwhelming - Jesus is always "on call" in case we need Him. His calming presence is there and if we'll just give in to it, He will lead us along His right paths.

And the Lord changed the wind to a very strong <u>west</u> wind
which caught up the locusts and carried them into the Red Sea.
Exodus 10:19

Vine

———§———

Father,

Because I am part of Your Vine, I know I must be cut back occasionally so I can grow more and reach out farther and farther. Sometimes it hurts, Father! Help me to bear it! Help me to accept Your pruning and trimming as part of my ongoing growth process. Remind me how much better I will be for it – and most of all, when I do bear a little fruit, don't let me preen and take the credit away from You. We branches only grow and produce because we are attached to The Mighty Vine!

I can plant an apple tree, Lord – I can nurture it and care for it by fertilizing and watering and pruning, but I still cannot produce the apples! The <u>tree</u> has to do that through the branches that are attached to the vine.

That example helps me remember that I cannot "produce" without You to help me, too. Help me to be like Your fruit as I spread Your good Word.

Remain in me, and I will remain in you.
No branch can bear fruit by itself; it must remain in me.
I am the vine; you are the branches. If a man remains in me and I in
Him, he will bear much fruit; apart from me you can do nothing.
John 15:4-5

Three Little Words...

———————— § ————————

THE BIBLE IS filled with information in the form of beautiful words and promises, and recently I noticed how some of the three-word phrases can trigger thoughts and ideas for us. Take time to think about these phrases and then think about the incidents leading up to them as well as the results of these three words. There may be only three words, but many of them tell a whole story.

Here are a few examples in the Old Testament:

Genesis 1:1	In the beginning.....
Exodus 16:4	Manna from heaven...
Ruth 16:1	Whither thou goest...
Ezekiel 37:7	bones came together

The following may be found in the New Testament:

Matthew 4:23	Teaching, preaching, healing...
Matthew 5:43	Love your neighbor...
Matthew 7:1	Do not judge...
Matthew 11:28	Come to me...
Matthew 11:29	Take my yoke...
Matthew 11:30	Burden is easy... yoke is light...
Matthew 6:11	Our daily bread...
Matthew 26:41	Watch and pray...
Luke 23:34	Father, forgive them...

John 1:29	Lamb of God…
John 1:14	Word became flesh…
John 11:43	Lazarus! Come out…
John 14:1	Trust in God… (also in me – go to prepare…)
John 14:17	Spirit of Truth…
John 15:4	Remain in me…
John 15:10	Obey my commands…
John 15:17	Love each other…
John 21:15(17)	Feed my lambs… (Feed my sheep…)
I Thessalonians 5:11	Encourage one another…

Peace

———— § ————

WHAT DO YOU think of when you hear the word "peace?" With our current world situations, most of us probably think of peace as an absence of war – an end to shootings and bombings and killings. The dictionary gives several definitions of peace. In addition to a treaty or agreement to end a war or to put hostilities aside, peace is described as serenity – calm – quiet. This kind of peace is also harmony, and an undisturbed state of mind. This makes me think of the peace I experienced when I took a ride in a hot air balloon. I don't believe I've ever been in the center of such pure, utter quiet – a true absence of sound of any kind. I felt that peace wash over my entire body as it enveloped me while I was up in the air.

In the Old Testament one of the words for peace is Shalom. Shalom was both a greeting and a farewell comment. It implied you were welcome in peace when you arrived, and you were wished continuing peace as you departed. Most of all, shalom speaks of a beautiful relationship with God. In the New Testament the word for peace is the Greek word "Eirene." It describes a new relationship – the relationship between God and His people.

Isaiah 26 speaks of peace as the result of a surrendered heart. In Philippians 4, Paul says peace is the result of a protected heart. True peace is not just tranquility. It is a quiet trust in God who <u>only</u> wants what is best for us. It is peace in the midst of a storm. Paul said, *"For God is a God not of disorder but of peace,"* and then in Colossians 3:15 he says, *"Let the peace of Christ rule in your hearts, since as members of one body you were called to peace. And be thankful."*

In Matthew Chapter 5 we find the Beatitudes and in verse 9 Jesus says, *"Blessed are the peacemakers for they will be called the sons of God."* The peace we find in this world is dependent upon time, place and circumstance. It comes and it goes. Jesus was talking about spiritual peace, the peace that only comes from God. He spelled it out for us again in John 14 when He said, *"Peace I leave with you; my peace I give you. I do not give to you as the world gives."*

One of the special blessings for us as Christians is peace – this peace of God. This is the peace all people desire, but no money can buy. This peace we carry within ourselves is God's gift. If we could earn a gift, it would no longer be a gift. I once read that the peace of God is God's own calm, restful heart possessing ours and filling us with His divine stillness. We must relinquish ourselves to God to experience this peace and this loving relationship with Him as our Lord and Savior.

A writer once said *"Sow the seed of peace and reap the harvest of quiet. The secret of peace, for one thing, is in prayer, which puts me in direct contact with the Prince of Peace."* He went on to say that peace does not dwell in outward things, but it dwells within the soul. He felt that peace in its truest and most powerful form is the pervasive influence of love expressed to others in good will, compassion, harmony, contentment and good cheer.

Peace can be the outgrowth of putting Christ as our first priority. It is the presence of the Lord in our hearts and our minds. It comes as the result of forgiving ourselves and then we can offer forgiveness to others. We cannot have peace <u>of</u> God until we are at peace <u>with</u> God. More importantly, this peace cannot be kept unless it is shared. We are not to <u>keep</u> peace, but to <u>make</u> peace – and then not to keep it, but to give it away. If we seek peace only for our own comfort, it will lose its purpose and it will be totally ineffective. We must remember that peace only comes as pride goes. If our minds are open to receive the divine presence of the risen Christ into our lives, He comes in, speaking peace. The Beatitudes verse does not say, *"Blessed are the peacekeepers...*" – it says *"blessed are the peacemakers."* James tells us in James 3:18 (LB) that the peacemakers will plant seeds of peace and reap a harvest of goodness. When you give of your possessions, you give very little. It is when you give of yourself that you truly give.

The night before His crucifixion Jesus' He left the disciples with words of peace. This is what I wish for each of us today and from this day forward – His true, deep, abiding peace.

> *"Peace I leave with you; my peace I give you.*
> *I do not give to you as the world gives.*
> *Do not let your hearts be troubled and do not be afraid."*
> *John 14:27*

Gratitude

———— § ————

THE DICTIONARY SAYS that gratitude is being thankful – It is a feeling of thankful appreciation for favors received. It is from the French word *gratus,* spelled with a u. The word gratis, spelled with an i, the next word in the dictionary alphabetically, is an adjective or adverb and it means without charge or payment. In other words, free. Backing up just a bit we come to the word "gratify." The meaning of that word is said to give pleasure or satisfaction. So – we can be grateful by expressing our gratitude to someone else – and that could cause that someone else to be gratified and then he or she could show gratitude to the next person they meet causing them to be grateful! It's ongoing! It's not a one-time thing! You could even say it's "catching" when it is shared! You can give it away, but you can still have it!

A writer once wrote that gratitude helps you grow and expand. She went on to say that gratitude brings joy and laughter into your life and into the lives of those around you. If you feel gratitude, and express gratitude, and it is appreciated and accepted, then that person will be in a state of gratification – and with any luck, they will pass it on again!

Holiday times can be a great time to express your gratitude to friends and family. You can do this by writing notes and cards, baking cookies, etc. You can also do things for those who are less fortunate and are in need. This kind of gratitude not only expresses our appreciation but it also demonstrates love and compassion for our fellow man.

Here are some more quotes I found about gratitude: The poet Marcel Proust wrote: *"Let us be grateful to people who make us happy; they are the charming gardeners who make our souls blossom."* Albert Schweitzer said this: *"At times our own light goes out and is rekindled by a spark from another person. Each of us has cause to think with deep gratitude of those who have lighted the flame within us."*

Oprah Winfrey was quoted as saying, *"Be thankful for what you have; you'll end up having more. If you concentrate on what you don't have, you will never, ever have enough."* Lastly, I found this one written by philosopher and psychologist William James: *"The deepest craving of human nature is the need to be appreciated."*

Starting today, let us go forth with an attitude of gratitude!

Be imitators of God, therefore, as dearly loved children and
live a life of love, just as Christ loved us and gave himself up for us
as a fragrant offering and sacrifice to God.
Ephesians 5:1-2

Time

––––– § –––––

TIME! THE DICTIONARY gives many interpretations and meanings for the word time. It is explained as "the duration in which things happen in the past, present and future – every minute there has been or ever will be." That's big! Think about it! Every minute there has been or ever will be. That means before us and after us! Time won't stop when we're no longer here. It will go on and on.

Time! It is a system of measuring the passing of hours – and days – etc. It is the period between two events and it separates periods in history. It can be a term of imprisonment, a term of apprenticeship, or a term of military service. Time is the appointed moment for something to happen – for something to begin or end. It is a precise instant – a minute, an hour, a day, a year, etc., determined by the clock or by the calendar. Time can describe a period of peace – or a time of war - or having a good time. We use time and timers in our kitchens constantly as we refer to recipes and to the time that something is to bake, broil, boil or simmer. It can also mean procrastination if we keep referring to "next time."

Time! It can also be a grouping of rhythmic beats into measures of equal length, as in a piece of music. An orchestra or band works together to make pleasurable music by playing in time to written music. A metronome is designed to "keep time." As an example, it helps a piano player keep the rhythm of a song at the pace intended by its composer.

Time! My Bible Concordance says it is a "continuum of past, present and future events." The book of Genesis refers to the time of creation. In

Ecclesiastes we hear that there is a time for everything and a season for every activity under heaven. In the New Testament, the Gospel writers refer to time being fulfilled with the coming of Jesus, the Christ Child. Later, in the Book of Ephesians Paul reminds us that when the time was right, God sent his one and only son to earth to be born of a woman that mankind might be saved. He later challenged the people of Ephesus to use their time wisely and well.

Today our job is to use our time and spend our time wisely so that in looking back, we won't feel we have wasted our time on something frivolous. We should take our time so we don't rush headlong into something we cannot handle. We are also to remember to be grateful for the time we have. Every evening we should thank God for our time that day.

When we say we haven't the time to do something it means that event or happening is not important enough at that time for us to use our time on it. We all have the same amount of time in our hours and days. When something is truly important to us, we will find the time to include it.

Let's be certain that we take the time to plan our time so we may use our time in ways pleasing to God. Remember, none of us knows how much time we have! Don't make the mistake of attempting to bank your time in hopes of gaining interest on it. Instead, go ahead and spend your time --- invest your time, but please do it wisely!

The Lord is a refuge and a stronghold in times of trouble. Psalm 9:9

Joy

THE DICTIONARY GIVES these definitions of the word joy: "A very glad feeling; happiness; delight." The word "joy" appears in the New Testament more than 60 times, and the words "joy," "joyful," and "gladness" appear in the Psalms over 90 times! As we go on here, you'll see how very important this feeling or idea was to our Lord Jesus Christ.

One writer said, "Joy doesn't come from desperate seeking – it comes as a result of self-surrender." To that I would add that it depends only on our personal relationship with Jesus Christ as our Savior and the Lord of our lives... And it depends on the fellowship we feel with Him that will then radiate out to others. Another writer said, *"The mark of a true Christian is, of course, love; but another mark is joy. It is the joy of overcoming, of victory through the positive power of Jesus Christ working, always working, in the mind – and demonstrating itself in the spirit – the undefeatable spirit."* And still another person said, *"The joy our Lord experienced came from doing what the Father sent him to do."* When children or grandchildren see no joy in the home, no joy in your Christianity, they will not be attracted by it. The best way to get a child to eat his food is for him to see his parents enjoying theirs! Our children will not be attracted to Christ if we make Him seem dull! Someone else once said, *"Joy is a net of love by which you catch souls."*

True joy is the outward evidence of God in our lives. It is impossible to really live in Jesus and not feel His joy flowing through us. During His life on earth, Jesus made many references to joy. One, in John 15, verse 11, says: *"These things I have spoken to you that my joy may be in you, and your joy may be full.*" From Jesus' words on joy we learn that joy is a two-fold proposition. He is saying that if we abide in Him and He abides in us, we will be able to live in the fullness of His joy. He wants us to take an inward pleasure in loving and serving Him – and He wants us to experience pleasure from loving and serving Him outwardly in our dealings with others.

Another person who often spoke of feelings of joy was Paul. He felt joy in his heart when he prayed for the Philippians. In Philippians 1:4 he says, *"In all my prayers for all of you, I always pray with joy."* I have a dear friend who signs her letters with her name followed by that verse – Phil. 1:4 – and when she does that, she fills ME with joy!

In Luke 12 the Lord promises US joy. He says this: *"There will be great joy for those who are ready and waiting for His return."* He goes on to say that He Himself will seat them and serve them. In Luke 15, Jesus relates several parables to His disciples. He speaks of the shepherd rejoicing when He finds one lost sheep and returns it to his flock. The woman who lost a coin swept every nook and cranny until she found it, and then she called in her friends and neighbors to rejoice with her. Jesus also said that there is joy in the presence of the angels of God when one sinner repents. Here are some other Bible verses that speak of joy.

1. Psalm 16:11 *"...in thy presence there is fullness of joy."*
2. Zephaniah 3:17 *"The Lord your God is with you, He is mighty to save. He will take great delight in you, He will quiet you with His love, He will rejoice over you with singing."* Isn't it a nice feeling to think we can do something that will make the Lord happy? All we need to do is to listen to Him and then respond!
3. Leviticus 9:24, *"Fire came out from the presence of the Lord and consumed the burnt offering and the fat portions on the altar. And when all the people saw it, they shouted for joy and fell facedown."* This was an example of Godly reverence for they were acknowledging God's Majesty. This came about after Moses and Aaron had been in the

Tent of Meeting after Moses summoned Aaron and his sons and the elders of Israel.

4. Nehemiah 8:10, *"...for the joy of the Lord is your strength."*
5. Luke 1:14-15a, *"He will be a joy and delight to you, and many will rejoice because of His birth, for He will be great in the sight of the Lord."* This was the Angel of the Lord speaking to Zechariah and Elizabeth about the son she was carrying, John the Baptist.

Someone once said that God is the Good Gardener who toils over us and tends us with constant care. He finds joy in the planting He has done, and He waits eagerly for a crop. With great joy He gathers the harvest. There is deep delight and enthusiasm in everything He undertakes. The instant I comply with His wishes, His joy energizes my being. The moment I disagree with His desires, joy fades and faith falters.

When you think of the word "Joy", think of it with this interpretation:

J is for Jesus who is to be first in our lives;
O is for others, for whom we must pray,
Y is for you.

If we put Jesus and others before ourselves, then we can share in and begin to experience true joy in our lives. Go in peace and in the joy of the Lord!

I have great confidence in you; I take great pride in you.
I am greatly encouraged; in all our troubles
my joy knows no bounds.
II Corinthians 7:4

Immediate Attention

———— § ————

Dear Lord,

What a wonderful feeling to know that when I need You and call on You, You will never put me on "hold!" You won't play tinny, loud music in my ears while You finish with someone else! And you won't ask me to leave my name and number so You can get back to me when you have time. Thank You, Father, that You are ALWAYS ready to give me your <u>undivided</u> attention <u>just</u> when I need it most!

Here I am! I stand at the door and knock.
If anyone hears my voice and opens the door, I will come
in and eat with him and he with me.
Revelations 3:20

(This verse tells me that WE have to open the door!
He will NOT come in without an invitation!)

Armor

——— ◊ ———

IN THE 6TH chapter of Ephesians as well as I Thessalonians, Paul tells us to be strong in the Lord and in His almighty power. He says we must stand firm, putting on the full armor of God. He goes on to mention a belt of truth buckled around our waist, a breastplate of righteousness on our chest, and our feet are fitted with the readiness that comes from the gospel of peace. He also speaks of wearing a helmet of salvation and our sword of the Spirit, which is the word of God.

Isn't it interesting that there is NO mention of a need for armor for the Christian's back! When you stand firm and face your problems, and God, you are protected, but if you turn away from God, or if you are running away and hiding from Him, your protection is gone!

But since we belong to the day, let us be self-controlled, putting on faith
and love as a breastplate, and the hope of salvation as a helmet.
I Thessalonians 5:9

Silence

———— § ————

THE DICTIONARY AND the Bible Concordance say that silence is the absence of any sound or noise – it is a stillness. It means to be free from sound or noise – no vocal or audible sound. The Thesaurus gives several words to substitute for silence: peace, hush, calm, and quiet. Each of these words conjure up a mental picture of silence. The dictionary also says it is a failure to communicate or to repress. This tells me that being silent may not always be the best thing! If we keep silent and fail to communicate our beliefs and communicate to others that God is in charge of our lives, we are being silent for the wrong reasons!

In Psalm 46:10 the Psalmist tells us we are to be still and know that the Lord is God. Zechariah 2:13 says almost the same thing. It says, *"Be still before the Lord because he is ready to judge."* These words say that if we are busy talking, we are not listening to God.

One Bible concordance adds another definition – secrecy. When we do not communicate or we do not speak out in favor of God, we are being silent for the wrong reasons. If we believe in something, we need to communicate that belief to those around us. We are told all through the Bible that we are to stand up for God's word. There are times we need to speak and not be silent because our silence could easily be misinterpreted. Ecclesiastes 3:7 tells us there is a time for everything and that includes a time to be silent, and a time to speak.

Habakkuk 2:20 says this: *"But the Lord is in his holy temple; let all the earth be silent before him."* The verses leading up to this speak of idols having no value even though man may have carved them. Idols cannot speak. Wood, gold and silver are silent because they have no breath and we cannot command them otherwise but in God's presence, we are to be silent, worshipful and completely respectful. When we come to God in prayer we are to praise him, we are to thank him, we are to make our requests known to him – and then <u>we</u> <u>are</u> <u>to</u> <u>be</u> <u>silent</u>! We are to listen to Him. We must remember that our God is a gentleman! He will not talk to us while we are talking! He asks that we be silent before Him so we can hear Him! When we are not talking while in God's presence, we are opening ourselves to ingesting His Word, to hearing His promises, and to learning His plans for us. Our silence in His presence indicates our willingness to trust, to learn, and to follow. Let us each strive for more of this "heavenly silence."

> *Even a fool is thought wise if he keeps silent,*
> *and discerning if he holds his tongue.*
> *Proverbs 17:28*

> *Be still, and know that I am God;*
> *I will be exalted among the nations,*
> *I will be exalted in the earth.*
> *Psalm 46:10*

Conductor

―――――§―――――

GOD STANDS BEFORE us as a conductor before an orchestra. We, the musicians, must keep our eyes on Him and on the music in front of us which represents our lives. Membership in His orchestra is open to everyone, but only the faithful and truly dedicated will make it through all the "readings" and "rehearsals." He may direct us to go high or low, or fast or slow. Rests are allowed each instrument throughout the song of life. Different instruments are featured and highlighted, but in the end all receive the applause and all are acknowledged and recognized. They each know they are important to the song of life, but they also appreciate the contributions of the others around them who provide the harmony or accent the melody. All who hear and all who play acknowledge the importance of the Conductor. Without Him we would have only discord and a total lack of harmony.

Let's willingly keep our eyes on this Conductor in our lives. That way we will follow His leadings and His direction which will help us to maintain both melody and harmony in our lives. By doing this, we are fulfilling God's wishes for us and we are sending out good vibes to those around us.

Live in harmony with one another. Do not be proud,
but be willing to associate with people of low position.
Do not be conceited.
Romans 12:16

Cynthia Irish Hockins

This is what the Lord says: "I am the Lord your God,
who teaches you what is best for you,
who directs you in the way you should go."
Isaiah 48:17

Promises

Dear Lord,

Your beautiful words are filled with so many beautiful promises. You make it plain and clear that You want only the best for me. I need only be willing to receive it and it is mine! With it comes a joy and inner glow that is difficult to put into words. It is a warmth that comes from way, deep inside me – and it grows and spreads through me as Your words come funneling in and speak to me personally.

You tell me over and over that Your love is steadfast and You will never leave me! Lord, remind me not to wander away from YOU! Often when I've felt lost or alone I've been tempted to blame You. Remind me, Father, that it is I who strayed, not You. You are right where you always promised You would be. Please help me get back on the right track! Forgive my wanderings. Pull me up as I climb and hold Your loving wings under me lest I fall. The rewards are so worth the effort!

Oh, Father, You were there ALL the time - - forgive me - - it was I who was away....

The Lord is not slow in keeping his promise,
as some understand slowness. He is patient with you,
not wanting any to perish, but everyone to come to repentance.
II Peter 3-9

Relationships

———— § ————

"When you are in the final days of your life, what will you want? Will you hug that college degree in the walnut frame? Will you ask to be carried to the garage so you can sit in your car? Will you find comfort in rereading your financial statement? Of course not. What will matter then will be people. If relationships will matter most then, shouldn't they matter most now?"

This statement by Max Lucado reminds me of something my Mother once wrote. In her last days she made a number of taped recordings talking about her early life and her family and relating what she knew about our Dad's family. I transcribed these tapes and then made copies for my brother and sister. They were in no particular date order – just thoughts as she remembered them – and a few things were repeated too. I enjoyed hearing her voice as I typed what she was saying, and it was most pleasant to hear her laughing or chuckling at certain times over some happy or funny memory. She prefaced this whole project with these words: *"People have been first in importance in my life, places have given me memories of happy and unhappy events, and things have always seemed least important but must creep into any account of one's experiences – so, for the most part, this record will deal with many people, a few places and only some things."*

The dictionary says this about the word relationship: It is a noun and it refers to the state or an instance of being related. It is a connection by blood or marriage; a kinship. We often hear of someone having a good relationship with someone else, or younger people may say they are "in a relationship" with someone which means they are dating and getting to know one another. In each of these instances, we WANT the relationship to be a good one – a positive one. This also describes our spiritual nature. Each of us should be in a relationship with the Triune God – Father, Son and Holy Spirit. As Christians, it is difficult to separate them.

As Max Lucado pointed out, in our final days we may find that all of our relationships really matter, so we should start improving and building on them right now! This not only refers to familial relationships but it refers to our personal relationship with Jesus Christ as our Lord and Savior. It's NEVER too late to work on that – it is an ongoing project and the more time we spend improving it, the easier it becomes and the closer that relationship becomes.

Any relationship can become stale or dull when it is taken for granted, personal or otherwise, but we are never too old to learn and never too old to try something new. With regard to your Christian relationship with God, your "Me and God time," why not challenge yourself to try something new and different for a few days. By doing this, you may decide you like this new approach and perhaps it will become a good habit! If what you try doesn't seem to satisfy you, change things around even more to suit you – but above all, don't sit back and give up too quickly. Don't stay in a "dull rut."

For example, if you start your day with prayer and then a devotion and perhaps some Bible reading, change it around and do your Bible reading first and then pray – and add some thoughts or some thanks for the verses or chapters you read before coming to God. Tell Him how the words you read spoke to you and how you felt about them – and tell Him how some phrase or verse or chapter may affect your day today. He likes to be thanked and praised regularly too, you know. Then finish up your "Me and God time" by reading a devotion.

God welcomes any kind of attention you are willing to give. You don't have to be on your knees to pray. You can pray anytime and anywhere. You can speak out loud or you can just think the words to yourself. You can be in your favorite chair or in your car or at your desk. (I often pray when I'm driving somewhere – sometimes mentally and sometimes out loud. Now, with all the hands-free phones I don't feel so silly if another driver sees me talking to myself!) You can pray while you are ironing or washing dishes or even pushing the vacuum cleaner. God knows the attitude of our hearts and that's what's really important! He is always willing to listen, no matter where we are or how we come to Him.

Rescue me and deliver me in your righteousness;
turn your ear to me and save me. Be my rock of ref-
uge, to which I can always go;
give the command to save me, for you are my rock and my fortress.
Psalm 71:2, 3

Choices

———— § ————

THANK YOU, LORD, for choices. That may seem like a small thing, but it is truly a big thing and I am thankful for it. I have choices to make every day in all that I do. I choose what clothes I will wear, what foods I will eat, what activities I will take part in, what people I will spend time with and how I will use my time.

You gave us so many examples of choice in The Bible. Moses had a choice – he chose to follow his people. Esther had a choice – she chose to help her fellow Jews. Daniel had a choice – he chose to follow your guidance, even into the lion's den. David had a choice – he chose adultery and then murder and then he sought and received forgiveness, and he repented.

I also have choices to make regarding Your place in my life. Help me to make the right choices, Father – to choose You over idleness – to choose Your Word over too much television or mindless novels – to choose Your commandments over daily temptations. Forgive me when my choices do not meet Your expectations and help me to do better the next time I'm faced with a choice.

I choose to be Your child, Lord. I choose to follow You and to make You the center of my life and not just a small, token part of it. Help me to follow through. . . . .

CHOICE = Christ Helps Our Ideals Center on Eternity

Teacups

COFFEE MUGS.... TEA cups... cups and saucers... I bet we all have some of each of these in our cupboards. At one time in my life I insisted that everything match – dishes, cups, saucers, etc. and I would never pour coffee into a cup unless it was sitting on a saucer. Over time my ideas have changed, and my collection has grown. I accumulated mugs and cups from my travels and they are now nice reminders of places I have visited and things I have seen. I've received many as gifts, too, and my "favorite" changes quite regularly now

One thing has not changed over the years and that's that I have a couple cups I only use for tea. There is no reason for that other than it's my own little fetish. I have a few cups & saucers that were gifts from my Dad before I was married, and I also have a few that belonged to my mother-in-law. Those have their special place in the china cabinet along with another of my favorite cups and saucers. That set is now almost 60 years old and it was a souvenir from a trip to Bermuda, b.c. (before children). I still marvel that it made the trip home with no chips or cracks, but as it has aged, and both pieces are now severely "crackled" so it is just to look at – but again, there are nice memories. My kids will probably discard them when I'm gone because they look old and they have no memories attached to that set except that it's always been in the china cupboard or a glass cabinet.

In thinking about that set and how fragile it has become, I remember reading about Jeremiah in the Old Testament. In Chapter 18 the Lord told him to go to a potter's house where he would receive a message. When he arrived the potter was shaping a pot with clay but the clay was marred, so using his hands, he mashed it all together and formed it into another pot. He could have thrown it away, or added new clay, but he chose to rework it. When he was finished the flaw was nowhere to be seen. He broke it down, reworked it, and then it was not only usable, it had become a thing of beauty.

Isaiah says this in Chapter 64:8: *"Yes, O Lord, you are our Father. We are the clay, you are the potter; we are all the work of your hand."* What a beautiful reminder for each of us today. He never discards us or "trades us in;" instead he waters us down. He never taking His hands or eyes off of us. He reworks us and reshapes us, and He makes us more usable – and more acceptable in His sight.

So, let me ask you now ….what shape are you in today? Are you chipped here and there? Do you feel like you've been battered around the sink a few too many times or tossed around in the dishwasher? Listen to this little short story I found telling about a teacup -- --

"A couple often went to England to shop in a beautiful antique store they found on a side street. This particular trip was to celebrate their 25th anniversary and they wanted something memorable to take home with them. They spotted an exceptionally pretty cup and saucer set and asked the proprietor if they could please hold it. As she handed it to them, the teacup suddenly spoke to them!

"'You don't understand," it said, "I have not always been a teacup. There was a time when I was just a lump of red clay. My master took me and rolled me, pounded and patted me over and over, and I yelled out, 'Don't do that! I don't like it! Leave me alone!' But he only smiled, and gently said, 'Not yet!'"

"'Then – wham! I was placed on a spinning wheel and I was spun around and around until I was terribly dizzy! I called out, but the master just nodded and quietly said, 'Not yet!' He spun me and he poked and prodded and bent me out of shape to suit himself and then…. He put me into the oven! Oh, I had never <u>felt</u> such heat! I yelled, I knocked, I pounded at the door. 'Get me <u>out</u> of here!' I shouted. I could see him and I could read his lips as he shook his head from side to side and said, 'Not yet!'

"'When I thought I couldn't bear it another minute, the door opened. He took me out very carefully and set me on the shelf and I began to cool. Oh, that felt SO good! After I cooled, he picked me up and he brushed me and painted me all over. The fumes stunk horribly! 'Oh, stop it!' I cried. But he only shook his head and said, 'Not yet!'

"Then <u>suddenly</u> I was back in the oven! Only it was not like the first time! This was <u>twice</u> as hot and I just <u>knew</u> I would suffocate! I begged, I pleaded, I screamed and I cried! I was convinced I would <u>never</u> make it! Just then, the door opened and he took me out and again, he carefully placed me on the shelf to cool and I waited – and I waited, wondering what could possibly happen next! An hour later he handed me a mirror and said, 'Look at yourself!' So I did. 'That can't be me!' I said. 'That's beautiful! Oh, my - now <u>I'm</u> beautiful!'

"Quietly he spoke to me. 'Remember this. I know it hurt being rolled, pounded and patted, but had I just left you alone, you would have dried up. I know it made you dizzy to spin on the wheel, but if I had stopped, you would have crumbled. I know it was hot and disagreeable in the oven, but if I hadn't put you there, you would have cracked.' He paused a minute, and then he went on to say, 'I know the fumes were bad when I brushed and painted you all over, but if I hadn't done that, you never would have hardened and you would not have had any color in your life. If I hadn't put you back in that second oven, you wouldn't have survived for long because the hardness would not have held. NOW you are a finished product. NOW you are what I had in mind when I first began with you.'"

The moral of this story? God knows what He is doing in each of us. He is the potter, and we are His clay. He will expose us to just enough pressures of just the right kinds so we may be made into a flawless in his eyes – and then we can fulfill His good, pleasing and perfect will for us. When life seems hard and you are being pounded and patted and pushed almost beyond endurance – when your world seems to be out of control – when you feel you are in a fiery furnace or when life seems to just plain "stink," try this. Boil some water and brew a cup of your favorite tea -- -- pour it into your prettiest teacup and sit down and think about this story -- -- and then, have a little talk with The Potter!

Excerpts from Hebrews 13:21: May the God of
peace equip you with everything good
for doing his will, and may he work in us what is pleasing to him.

Manna

———— ◊ ————

WHEN THE ISRAELITES were in the wilderness, they needed food and sustenance daily and they voiced their concerns to their leader, Moses. They feared they would starve to death, but the Lord told Moses He would take care of the needs of the people, and indeed, He did just that! Each day when they arose, they found manna on the ground nearby. There was always ample for each one according to his needs. Isn't that a lot like God's Word today? He provides that for us too, in the form of The Bible, and its words are provided according to our needs. We can partake of it daily and it gives us strength and nourishment each day.

The Israelites had to go out each morning and gather their own manna. No one did it for them. It had to be gathered each day and could not be stored ahead for later. We cannot "store up" God's Word either. We need to delve into it and read it each day for renewal and revitalization as we begin our day. Each day has its own message and words of enlightenment that are appropriate for that time in our lives. If we are not "in the Word," we may miss a blessing!

Manna was considered the "bread of life" to the Israelites. Christ said that He is our daily bread now and He proved that by giving us His Word to nourish and complete us.

Have you had YOUR manna today?

*So they asked him, "What miraculous sign then will you give
that we may see it and believe you? What will you do?
Our forefathers ate the manna in the desert; as it is written: 'He gave
them bread from heaven to eat.'"
"I tell you the truth, it is not Moses who has given you the bread
from heaven, but it is my Father who gives you the true
bread from heaven. For the bread of God is he
who comes down from heaven and gives life to the world."
John 6:30-33*

Show and Tell

Dear Father,

You bring me such joy, Lord! Most of the time You don't even need to say a word! Just knowing You are here with me brings me great joy!

True joy doesn't depend on circumstances or on surroundings. Joy depends only on my relationship with You – Jesus Christ – as my Savior and the Lord of my life. Your words in John tell me You want Your joy to be in all of us and you want our joy to be full. That must mean You want us to be full to overflowing and You want us to be <u>filled</u> with you!

We can't really live in you and with you and not experience that joy, Father. It is an indescribable feeling – and if it is there, we'll know it! We can't <u>see</u> joy, but we will <u>feel</u> it and as we <u>feel</u> joy, help us to show it so others will know it's there and also that it's available to them too!

I thought I was too old for Show and Tell, Father, but this proves I'm not!

I have told you these things that my joy and delight
may be in you, and that your joy and gladness
may be full measure and complete and overflowing.
John 15:11 (Amplified)

Trust

THE DICTIONARY HAS numerous definitions for the word trust. Trust can be a firm belief in another's reliability. It is also a confident, hopeful expectation. It can explain a kind of care or custody of something or someone. When that is how the word is used, a person then becomes a trustee – one who is in control and who has been appointed to manage and see to the needs of another.

God put His trust in His Son, Jesus. Jesus then became our Trustee. He shows this by His ongoing care and concern for our well-being and our welfare. When we submit ourselves to Him, it means we are allowing Him to be in control of us – to care for us – to guide and direct us in all our ways throughout all of our lives. He continuously meets our needs because of this mutual trust. Unless we trust in someone outside ourselves and someone bigger than ourselves, the world can seem like a scary place. We will feel a special peace when we submit ourselves to God and His teachings and His will for each of us.

Thank heaven for our trusting God and also for our Trustee, Jesus! A trusting faith is the key to God's Kingdom. No amount of education or scholastic achievement can equal the satisfaction we can feel by enjoying a trusting relationship with God.

"I will put my trust in Him."
Isaiah 8:17 and Hebrews 2:13

"O Lord Almighty, blessed is the man who trusts in you."
Psalm 84:12

"It is better to trust in the Lord than to put confidence in man."
Psalm 118:8(KJV)*

*It has been said that this verse is the middle verse in the Bible, and the words "the Lord" are the middle two words in that verse! What beautiful planning!

Enduring and Endearing

———— § ————

I HAVE ALWAYS been interested in words of all kinds. I seem to be especially drawn to words or phrases that sound alike or where the spellings are close. These are two words that came to me recently so I spent some time checking them out.

To endure.... When we endure something it implies we are holding up under pain, fatigue, stress or duress – we are putting up with whatever it is. We are tolerating a situation, often because we don't really have a choice. My Bible Concordance says that to endure is to remain firm under suffering or misfortune. It also says there can be a blessing in the act of enduring. In II Timothy 2:10 the Living Bible quotes Paul as saying *"I am more than willing to suffer if that will bring salvation and eternal glory in Christ Jesus to those God has chosen."* A couple verses later Paul adds, *"And if we think that our present service for him is hard, just remember that some day we are going to sit with him and rule with him."*

Jesus endured many things during His years on this earth, especially in His last few years as He began His teachings and His travels. He endured false accusations from his enemies; he endured the humiliation of His arrest at Gethsemane; His trial, and His march to the cross wearing a crudely formed crown of thorns. He endured His long, slow, painful death on the cross. We should always be mindful of the fact that He not only endured all of these things, but He endured all of it quietly and with an air of acceptance and finality because He had long known His final fate.

To endear.... The word endear or endearing does not appear in my Concordance so it probably is not in the Bible, but I checked the dictionary and it says that when we say something (or someone) is endearing, we are expressing affection and a warm liking. We are saying that thing or that person is very dear to us – a precious treasure that we cherish greatly and consider beloved.

I immediately thought of Jesus when I read that. I consider Jesus to be very endearing. Because He endured all that He did, He is my treasure and I cherish the relationship I am enjoying with Him as I go about my life here on earth. Should there come a time, or an event, or a situation that I must endure, I know that our dear Lord will help me and He will hold me up. He has already demonstrated that endurance to me through the illnesses and losses of loved ones, and the loss of a number of dear friends. He was also with me through some serious personal illnesses and I constantly felt his presence. I bet each one of us can truly say His endearing and constant love and support has helped us to endure in similar situations! Let's remember to thank God for His love, His devotion, and for this gift of peace that passes all understanding.

Jesus Christ is the same yesterday and today and forever.
Hebrews 13:8

And the peace of God, which transcends all understanding,
will guard your hearts and your minds in Christ Jesus.
Philippians 4:7

Finished - Done

———— § ————

THE DICTIONARY DEFINES "done" as something that is completed or "sufficiently cooked." The word "finish" means to bring to an end – to complete – to use up or consume entirely. From this, I would surmise that something that is done (sufficiently cooked) can also be finished (used up or totally consumed). I can remember sitting at the kitchen table as a youngster and being told I'd have to remain there until I'd finished my dinner and my plate was empty (My parents were strong advocates of the "clean-your-plate-club and later my husband was too!) I can also recall being asked if I had done my homework or my piano practicing – and I often replied that yes, I had finished them.

Finish can also mean to render something as worthless or useless. To finish off is to end or destroy something and to finish with something can mean an end to relationships. You have finished sewing a garment when it's ready to wear and you have finished setting the table when it is ready for company. These examples show that at times these words can be used interchangeably. When I checked in my Bible Concordance under done, it also said "see completed, finished."

I enjoyed checking the many references to finished or completed in the Bible. Genesis 2:1 says, *"Thus the heavens and the earth were completed in all their vast array."* The 2nd verse goes on to say that by the seventh day God had finished the work he had been doing; so on the seventh day he rested from all his work.

A little later in I Kings, chapter 6, we are told that Solomon built the house (the temple) and finished it. In Zechariah, chapter 4, the Lord is speaking to Zechariah when he says, *"Zerubbabel helped rebuild the temple at Jerusalem. His hands laid the foundation of this temple and his hands will also complete it."*

Still later, in the New Testament in John 5, Jesus said, *"For the very work that the Father has given me to finish, and which I am doing, testifies that the Father has sent me."* He is saying He came for a purpose and He will follow through and finish it. Later in John 17 Jesus is praying to God after giving private instructions to His disciples just before His arrest in the Garden of Gethsemane. Here He says to His Father, *"I have brought you glory on earth by completing the work You gave me to do."* Still later, in John 19:30 we find the most famous use of the word finished. Jesus, after hanging on the cross for hours, said *"It is finished."* With that, He bowed His head and gave up His spirit.

In II Timothy chapter 4 Paul spoke to Timothy, his helper. He said, *"I have fought the good fight; I have finished the race; I have kept the faith. Now there is in store for me the crown of righteousness which the Lord himself will award to me."* What a beautiful way for him to sum up all that he had done in the name of the Lord. Isn't it great to hear him happily anticipating the award he is certain awaits him when he reaches heaven and stands before God? We should make every effort to follow his example so that someday we, too, may stand before God and receive that same kind of reward for finishing and completing the challenges we faced in our lives to His full and complete satisfaction.

Pathways

—— § ——

RECENTLY I HAD a conversation with a friend about someone whose address is on a <u>lane</u>. The person I was talking with lives on a <u>court</u>. This got me to thinking about all the different words used to describe a person's residential address, so I looked up some of these in the dictionary to try and differentiate between their various meanings. Then I began thinking about these words in relation to my Christian walk with God.0

A <u>road</u> is described as a way made for traveling between places by auto, horseback, etc. It is a path or a course, and it implies going somewhere. I <u>am</u> traveling between homes right now -- my earthly home and my eventual eternal home in Heaven, so I could be said to be on a road. That might not be all bad.

A road can also be called an <u>avenue</u>, and an avenue is a path, road, or drive, often bordered with trees. It is a way of approach to something or somewhere. That sounds nice, although perhaps a bit busy. I could be said to be on an avenue too.

An avenue can also be called a <u>boulevard</u>. A boulevard sounds regal and it is described as a broad street, often lined with trees, and often with a land-scaped island separating the driving lanes. So, as long as I'm on this trip, I might as well strive to be on a boulevard because it sounds peaceful and lovely.

Now a boulevard can also be a <u>street</u>. A street is described as a public road in a city or town. It is often a paved thoroughfare with sidewalks and buildings along each side. That would seem to describe a settled area – and since I enjoy people, I could also be said to be on a street for my journey.

A street can also be called a <u>lane</u>. A lane is described as a narrow way between hedges, walls, etc. – or a narrow road or street. Another description says a lane isn't really bound anywhere in particular. It implies being in no hurry to get where you're going and it often curves and winds around. That could be frustrating at times. Then again, it can also be any of the parallel courses marked off for contestants in some kind of a race. Well, I'm not sure I like the idea of being in a "marked off" area like that – and I don't want to feel confined to staying in my own lane and not having contact with others around me. I don't like thinking of my life as a race either – so I don't think I want to be on a lane. It sounds somewhat remote and almost lonesome.

A <u>court</u> is described as a short street, often closed at one end. Well, I don't want to be stuck like that. It sounds much too confining. That's a lot like a <u>cul-de-sac</u> which only has one outlet. It's also like a <u>place</u> which is a short street. These all sound like dead ends. I want to be able to grow in my relationship – to reach out and compare notes and to get encouragement from fellow Christians. These are obviously not the places for me! I'm not sure a <u>terrace</u> would work either. That is described as a row of houses on ground that is raised from the street. I might never have contact with the person at the opposite end of the row in this situation.

There were lots of meanings given for a <u>drive</u>, but the main one said it was a road for automobiles. Again, this seems to imply speed and moving fast and I don't want to go TOO fast because I could miss something important…. I could miss something I really need to focus on or that I should be incorporating into my lifestyle.

Well, I've covered a lot of these examples, but I think I've saved the best two for last. How about a <u>circle</u>? That implies a connection, one to another. It can refer to something that has no end, and that implies a type of security.

We have that security when we believe in Jesus as the Son of God and our Lord and Savior. I'm all for that kind of security!

The other one I saved is a <u>highway</u>. The dictionary says a highway is the "direct way." I certainly want a direct relationship with the Lord, and a highway gives me direct access to Him and to what He feels is best for me in my life's journey. A highway is filled with signs telling us which way to go; there are rest stops when we need to refresh and regroup; and reminders of where we are. They tell us what's just up ahead as well as what might be a long way down the road. These are the kinds of directions I want to follow!

I've given this a lot of thought and I've made my decision! I want to be on the <u>Highway to Him</u>!

Your word is a lamp to my feet, and a light for my path.
Psalm 119:105

The path of the righteous is level;
O upright One, you make the way of the righteous smooth.
Isaiah 26:7

Temptations

─────── ◊ ───────

O Lord,

I see more temptations! Everywhere I turn there are temptations! I know that by themselves temptations are not bad – it's what I DO with them and how I respond to them that makes the difference. Thank You for reminding me that through these temptations I always have a choice! Thank You for the feeling of strength and for making me stand just a little taller when I do NOT give in to a temptation! I know it's not me, Father – it's You working in me!

That discipline isn't always there, Lord. You know that better than anyone! Please forgive me when I DO give in. The momentary pleasure is not worth the long-term pain, but still, sometimes I do the wrong things. Help me to be more disciplined and remind me to stop and think…

Maybe I will make a list of the things that tempt me most often and beside it I'll make another column. That one I will title DENIALS and I'll write it down every time I do not give in and I'll follow it with a big thank you! Help me as each list grows, Lord. Help me to see the Denials list growing and the Temptations list shrinking. I can do it if we work together!

No temptation has seized you except what is common to man.
And God is faithful; he will not let you be tempt-
ed beyond what you can bear.
But when you are tempted, he will also provide a way out
so that you can stand up under it.
I Corinthians 10:13

Fall Trees

Dear Heavenly Father,

The trees are truly rejoicing as they preen and flaunt their glorious fall colors. You do marvelous things for us in giving us such awesome beauty everywhere we look at this time of year. You have turned batches of bright green trees into breathtaking groups of ambers, golds and crimsons. Thank You for reminding us that You are all powerful! You can do <u>anything</u>, and You want us to enjoy what You have given us.

Let us never take our surroundings for granted, dear Lord. Trees are constant reminders that we are to accept and enjoy what You provide and that we can also look for changes in our lives that are directed by Your wonderful, loving hands. Lord, each tree you speak of in the Bible is different from the others and each is the work of Your hands! Your wonders are so awesome! Thank you!

Then the trees of the woods shall rejoice be-
fore the Lord. I Chronicles 16:33

Beatitudes

—— ∮ ——

THE BEAUTIFUL BEATITUDES can be found in Matthew, Chapter 5 beginning with verse 3.

> *Blessed are the poor in spirit, for theirs is the kingdom of heaven.*
> *Blessed are those who mourn, for they will be comforted.*
> *Blessed are the meek, for they will inherit the earth.*
> *Blessed are those who hunger and thirst for righ-*
> *teousness, for they will be filled.*
> *Blessed are the merciful, for they will be shown mercy.*
> *Blessed are the pure in heart, for they will see God.*
> *Blessed are the peacemakers, for they will be called the sons of God.*
> *Blessed are those who are persecuted because of righ-*
> *teousness, for theirs is the kingdom of heaven.*
> *Blessed are you when people insult you, persecute you and*
> *falsely say all kinds of evil against you, because of me.*
> *Rejoice and be glad, because great is your reward in heaven,*
> *for in this same way they persecuted the prophets who were before you.*

The word "Beatitude" is not found anywhere in the Bible. It comes from the Latin word "beatus," which is the equivalent of the Greek word for "blessed" or happy. The Beatitudes are statements of fact. In His own words, Jesus attributes a state of blessedness to those whose lives contain or demonstrate certain qualities – and He gives the reason for this blessedness. Blessedness is such a condition as to create the consciousness of three things: (1) perfect peace, (2) perfect joy, and (3) perfect rest.

One example of perfect peace is mentioned in John 14:27 where Jesus says: *"Peace I leave with you, my peace I give you."* In the explanatory notes in my NIV Bible it says that all true peace is His gift. His peace is real and it is present.

Next is perfect joy, and this kind of joy is explained in John 15:11. Jesus says, *"I have told you this so that my joy may be in you and that your joy may be complete."*

Lastly, perfect rest is mentioned in Matthew 11:28. Jesus says, *"Come to me, all who*

are weary and burdened, and I will give you rest."

The first four Beatitudes speak of the poor in spirit, the sorrowing, meekness and hungering, and these indicate a state of <u>destitution</u> – a lacking or something that is missing and no longer there. The poor in spirit are in a condition of want. Those who mourn could refer to us when we recognize our condition. The meek could refer to our feeling when we acknowledge how lacking we are, and the hungering could refer to us when we seek to rectify our situation.

The next four Beatitudes speak more about a state of <u>restitution</u> – restoring and returning to a former, more acceptable condition. They talk of mercy, leniency, being pure in heart, being a peacemaker, and of being rewarded if persecution or harassment is due to speaking out for the Lord.

We are merciful when we forgive, and this is how God treats us when we come to Him in the right state of mind. The pure in heart are demonstrating their desire for restoration. Peace is our goal when we show mercy and become more pure in heart, and our reactions to being persecuted for speaking out for the Lord are different from our reactions to worldly persecutions or accusations.

Although these Beatitudes are listed in the book of Matthew, which is in the New Testament, there are also references in the Old Testament that use some of these same phrases. Isaiah 64:6 says all of us have become like one who is unclean and all our righteous acts are like filthy rags. It says we all shrivel up like a leaf, and like the wind our sins sweep us away. In Psalm 51:3 & 4, David acknowledges his sins and transgressions and he asks for forgiveness and for cleansing. With reference to hungering and thirsting after righteousness in the 4th beatitude, look at Psalm 42. These are favorite verses of mine. *"As the deer pants for streams of water, so my soul pants for you, O God. My soul thirsts for God, for the living God."*

Someone once said that the Beatitudes apply the Old Testament revelation to the entire race of mankind. They accomplish this, not by replacing the Old Testament, but in a sense The Beatitudes complete the Old Testament. With this completion, they extend its application and its implications into New Testament times and then even to the present day. You might say that through the Beatitudes God tells us the attitudes of our hearts are more important to Him than any service we can render in His name. Our attitudes influence others, for good or bad, and that places all the more importance on how God is reflected through us.

The Beatitudes comprise only a few verses, but they are filled with blessings and with promises that are there for all of us. We are all promised the kingdom of heaven. We are all promised comfort and mercy. We are all promised that we shall see God and that we will be called the sons and daughters of God. These are beautiful words that we can all cling to and rely on to strengthen us and increase our joy during the good times and to help us endure through the bad times.

In everything, do to others what you would have them
do to you, for this sums up the Law and the Prophets.
Matthew 7:12

The Lord's Prayer

———— § ————

THROUGH THE YEARS, enough has been written about The Lord's Prayer to fill volume after volume. Scholars all over the world have tried to interpret its true meaning, its deeper meaning, and explanation after explanation has mainly proved one thing to be true. It is a very simplistic prayer written for all – for the highly educated and the hardly educated. It was written with one goal in mind, and that was a prayer for all mankind. This prayer originally came about because the disciples went to Jesus and said, "Lord, teach us to pray." The Lord's Prayer came about as the result of this request. Jesus gave this prayer to them as a group – not to each individually.

First of all, please notice that nowhere in this prayer does the word "I" appear. There are NO singular mentions. All the phrases are plural. To me, this indicates that we are always to think of others when we pray, and it even recommends praying together. Jesus used words and phrases that would be familiar to the disciples and easy for them to understand and remember. These were not learned, schooled men – these were simple men from all kinds of everyday walks of life, so He spoke in words they could all understand.

The Lord's Prayer has a total of 68 words and none are over 3 syllables – and there are only two words that do have 3 syllables: hallowed and temptation. The Prayer is divided into 2 parts, and each part has 3 petitions. The first 3 have to do with God – with hallowing His name and seeking His Kingdom. The next 3 petitions have to do with our needs. (Remember, God first, then us.) Jesus began the prayer with "Our Father" to remind us that this prayer is a family matter, but this Father is in Heaven. Did you know that in the entire Old Testament, God is referred to as Father only 6 times? In the Gospels, which together are only a small fraction of the length of the Old Testament, Jesus speaks of "my father" or "our Father" more than <u>60 times</u>! Jesus recognized that a father gives life. He is a provider and a protector of the family.

The first half of the Lord's Prayer is designed to instruct because it deals with the concerns of God. When we turn to the Lord in prayer and involve ourselves in His concerns first, somehow our own personal problems begin to shrink. We begin to see His perspective and we automatically open ourselves to His presence.

In Matthew 11:29-30, Jesus speaks and asks us to learn from Him. He says His yoke is easy and His burden is light. If I am yoked with Jesus, His yoke is easy on me only if I am going in the same direction HE is going. Yoked animals work together and share the load because it's easier that way! In the end, it is far more productive.

When we say, "Give us this day," etc., keep in mind that Jesus chose those words carefully to teach us that the Lord God is the sole source of supply for everything we need. Also note that it says "this day." Too often we spend time being concerned or worrying about tomorrow – or next week. This doesn't mean we are not to plan ahead, it simply means we are not to be preoccupied with the future to the extent that "this day" is forgotten. Manna was given to the Israelites in the wilderness each day and for that day only. It could not be saved or stored up ahead of time because it turned rotten and moldy after the first day. God was providing for their needs as they needed them.

Then there is the phrase, *"Help us when we are tempted."* He does not say we won't be tempted, but when we are tempted, we are to ask for strength to turn away from it. We are asking God to help us beat down the devil when he tries to worm his way into our lives.

When Jesus tells us to say *"Forgive us our trespasses,"* etc., let's remember that this is conditional! We are asking for forgiveness so we may also forgive those who trespass against us. There's a clear connection here between our vertical relationship with God and our horizontal relationship with people. Note that these two relationships form a cross!

"Thine is the kingdom..." When we say this, we are saying we want HIM to be Lord of our lives! We cannot glorify God on our own terms. This can only be accomplished by doing His will.

When we close our prayer, we say Amen. Amen is a Greek word that translates to "verily" or "truly." An English translation might be "let it be so" or "so be it." We think of Amen as an ending, but is it really?

Let's remember as we praise Him, as we seek first His Kingdom, as we trust Him for our every need, as we receive forgiveness, as we triumph through life's temptations, because He is working out all the details of our lives, and all to His purpose! Each of our hearts contains a "Big 3" – me, myself and I. With just a little effort – and a lot of prayer! – and help from our Heavenly Father, those could easily be replaced, and our hearts could be filled with Father, Son and Holy Spirit! As we pray, let's ask God to take away the "self" in us and to replace it with more of Himself!

But God has surely listened and heard my voice in prayer.
Praise be to God, who has not rejected my prayer
or withheld his love from me!
Psalm 66:19, 20

Exceptional Women

———— § ————

ALL THROUGH THE Bible there are beautiful examples of exceptional women who were called upon or who volunteered to make a difference. Most of these women began their lives very simply, but each became a woman who took a step out in faith when God spoke or encouraged her in some way.

Miriam was the sister of Moses and Aaron. One of the meanings of her name is "strong," and she was strong when she needed to be. Miriam was a prophetess who was chosen and called by God. She was one of the accepted leaders of the people of her time. In Micah, Chapter 6, the Lord was speaking to the people of Israel when He said, "I sent Moses to lead you, also Aaron and Miriam." In Exodus 15:20 Miriam took a tambourine in her hand and all the women followed her with tambourines and dancing as she sang a victory song saying "the Lord is highly exalted." She didn't always follow God's plan and at one point she was punished by becoming a leper, but she was later cured. She died much later at Kadesh.

The name Ruth means "friendship or companion." She was both a friend and a companion to Naomi. Ruth the Moabite, a widow, took a step out in faith when she announced she would leave her homeland and travel to Bethlehem to live with and care for Naomi, her mother-in-law, who was also a widow. She embraced Naomi's God and was later rewarded with a marriage to Boaz. That marriage produced a son named Obed who became the father of Jesse. Jesse was the father of King David. She is one of the few women named in the lineage of Jesus. What a beautiful reward she received!

Rahab was called a woman of easy virtue who lived in Jericho. She agreed to hide 2 Israelite spies and in return her house and family were spared when Jericho was ransacked in the 6th chapter of Joshua. Her hospitality was rewarded in a big way! She is also one of the few women mentioned in the genealogy of Jesus and she is listed in Hebrews 11:31 as a woman of faith. What an honor for her!

Eunice and Lois are both mentioned in the book of II Timothy. Paul wrote to Timothy and spoke of Eunice, Timothy's mother and Lois, his grandmother. Paul said Lois, whose name means "pleasing," was a devout woman of Lystra. These women were teachers who nurtured Timothy and encouraged him in his work with Paul and in his devotion to Jesus Christ.

Dorcas, also called Tabitha, was a Christian woman of Joppa. Dorcas is mentioned in the Book of Acts. Her name means "gazelle." She served the sick and the poor and it was said that her heart was an "open door." Acts 9:36 describes her as a "good woman" whose charity and loyalty knew no bounds. When she became ill and died her body was washed and placed in an upstairs room. The disciples were called and Peter was taken upstairs to her room where all the widows stood around crying and showing him robes and other clothing the seamstress Dorcas had made. Peter listened and then he sent the women out of the room so he could kneel and pray. He turned toward the dead woman and said, "Tabitha, get up!" She opened her eyes and he helped her to her feet and all the women came in to see her and they were amazed and spread the word all through Joppa.

At one time, Mary Magdalene was possessed of seven demons until Jesus called the demons out of her and healed her. She was one of the women present at Jesus' crucifixion according to Matthew 27:56. A few verses later Matthew says she watched the stone rolled in front of the entrance of the tomb after His body had been wrapped in clean linen and placed there. Early the next day Mary Magdelene went to the tomb and found an angel sitting on the stone that had rolled away from the door to the tomb. The angel told Mary Magdelene Jesus had risen from the dead and the tomb was empty. She hurried away, filled with joy, to tell His disciples and suddenly Jesus was in front of her! She was the first person to see Him following his resurrection! He told her not to be afraid but to go and tell His brothers to go to Galilee where they would see Him also. She was truly blessed!

Lydia is only referred to a couple times in the Bible – in Acts 16, and again later for tending to the needs of Paul & Silas when they were in prison, but Paul included her in his writings. Lydia was an influential businesswoman in the city of Thyatira who dealt in purple cloth. This city was famous for its dyeing works, especially royal purple, which was in great demand by the upper classes. A group of women gathered at the river outside the city gates of Philippi. There were so few Jews in Philippi that there was no synagogue so the Jews who were there would meet along the banks of the river. On his travels, Paul spoke there and one who listened that day was Lydia, a worshiper of God. The Lord opened her heart to respond to Paul's message and she and all the members of her household were then baptized by Paul. In a spirit of hospitality, she invited Paul to come and stay at her house before he traveled further.

In Miriam we see strength and leadership. In Ruth we see humility and compassion. In Rahab we see a protector who helped save her family from death. In Lois and Eunice we see encouraging, devoted teachers. In Dorcas we see a seamstress who sewed for others. In Mary Magdelene we see a grateful follower of Jesus Christ. In Lydia we see a businesswoman who opened her heart to the Lord and her home to others. None of these women started out with the intention of "making a name for herself." As the Lord needed them and called them, they obeyed and each was rewarded for her willingness to serve, to lead, and step out in total faith to do as the Lord asked. We never know what the Lord may require of us to fulfill His will, but the wise woman listens and prays, and keeps herself ready!

Cynthia Irish Hockins

She sets about her work vigorously;
her arms are strong for her tasks.
Proverbs 31:17

Bible Emergency Numbers

———— § ————

THIS IS A handy list of "emergency numbers" in the Bible that could help you through some tough, trying times. Keep it handy! No operator assistance is required and all lines to Heaven are open 24 hours a day! You will never be put on hold!

When you are lonely or fearful	Call on Psalm 23
If you are depressed	Call Psalm 27
If people seem unkind	Call John 15
For assurance	Call Mark 8:35
For Paul's secret to happiness	Colossians 3:12-17
If you want to be fruitful	Call John 15
For understanding your Christianity	Call II Corinthians 5:15-19
When you have sinned	Call Psalm 51
For reassurance	Call Psalm 145:18
For security	Call Psalm 121:3
When you want peace and rest	Call Matthew 11:25-30
When you need courage for a task	Call Joshua 1
If you are in danger	Call Psalm 91
When you travel	Call Psalm 121
If your pocketbook is empty	Call Psalm 37
How to get along with others	Call Romans 12
If self-pride takes hold	Call Psalm 19

Cynthia Irish Hockins

When you feel down and out	Call Romans 8:31
If you are growing bitter	Call I Corinthians 13
When God seems far away	Call Psalm 139

Just close your eyes, dial, and listen for the answers – and remember if you feed your faith regularly, doubt will starve to death!

Jesus Outdoes Santa Claus

—— ⸓ ——

Santa lives at the North Pole.

JESUS is everywhere.

Santa rides in a sleigh.

JESUS is everywhere and He walks on water.

Santa comes but once a year.

JESUS is always present.

Santa fills your stockings with goodies.

JESUS supplies <u>all</u> your needs.

Santa comes down your chimney

JESUS stands at your door and knocks, uninvited and then enters your heart.

You stand in line and wait your turn to see him.

JESUS is as close as the mention of His name.

Santa lets you sit on his lap.

JESUS lets you rest in His arms.

Santa asks your name.

JESUS knew our name before we did and our address, our history, our future and even the hairs on our head.

Santa has a belly like a bowl full of jelly.	JESUS has a heart full of love.
All Santa can offer is HO HO HO	JESUS offers hope, health, and help.
Santa says "You better not cry."	JESUS says "Cast all your cares on me" and "I will save your tears in a bottle."
Santa's little helpers make toys.	JESUS gives new life and mends wounded hearts.
Santa may make you smile or chuckle.	JESUS gives you true inner joy that is your strength.
Santa puts gifts under your tree.	JESUS became our gift and died on a tree.

Obviously, there is really no comparison if **we** remember WHO Christmas is all about.

We need to keep Christ in Christmas. Jesus is still the reason for the season.

Vines

—— § ——

IN THE BOOK of John in the Bible, John talks about Jesus being the Vine and God being the Vinedresser. John starts out by quoting Jesus as saying, *"I am the true vine, and my Father is the gardener. He cuts off every branch in me that bears no fruit while every branch that does bear fruit, he prunes so that it will be even more fruitful."* Then Jesus speaks these challenging words by saying, *"Remain in me, and I will remain in you. No branch can bear fruit by itself; it must remain in the vine. Neither can you bear fruit unless you remain in me."*

Jesus repeats these words several times. I learned years ago that anytime something is repeated in the Bible, it is for emphasis and it is there for a reason! God is drawing special attention to these words and phrases by repeating them so we cannot miss His meaning. He says that each of us is expected to bear fruit, or else! We don't all bear the same fruit, or the same amount of fruit, but each of us is responsible for bearing <u>some</u> fruit!

Think about a vine for a moment. The natural vine thrives only when all parts of it are healthy – in balance – in harmony – each submitting to the vinedresser who cares for the whole vine. This enables it to fulfill its potential of fruit production. We cannot give up this responsibility without serious consequences! The vinedresser sees that the whole plant flourishes and at the same time glorifies God in its fruitfulness – but this only happens when each part is in a healthy, personal relationship with the other parts. All parts must work together for the common good.

When a vine is thriving, we see the fruit and the leaves, but the hidden parts – the roots, small tendrils, the sap, and the chlorophyll molecules –are all vitally important. We don't see them, but if they are not there it is evident because the vine will wither. If one branch on a vine is pruned incorrectly, infection can enter. That infection can spread to the whole plant! In our Christian fellowship, if one person yields to mistaken teachings, there can be repercussions throughout the whole community of Christians! It is only as each branch abides in Jesus, the Vine, that it can help the other branches grow and become stronger. It is our love for our fellow branches – particularly tender, new branches – that enables them to become coupled and filled with God's wisdom.

God has also proclaimed a dormant period for all tender shoots to allow for some quiet, inner growth. It is important not to press new Christians into trying to bear fruit before they are ready. God has a perfect timetable for each of us in this respect. A new branch cannot bear fruit until it is strong enough to bear its own weight. If it is given too much weight to carry, it will break. New, young fruit must be allowed to ripen and to develop slowly into full maturity. It needs time to fit into the unique plan God has for it. Pray for guidance and for wisdom during any "dormant period" as you strive to grow in Christ and bear fruit for Him.

The fruit of the righteous is a tree of life,
and he who wins souls is wise.
Proverbs 11:30

Christmas

CHRISTMAS! THE THEME and the emphasis of Christmas should be on the giving and not on the getting. Unless we focus on others at this time, our holidays – and maybe even our hearts – will be as empty as Herod's soul. The real expression of Christ in Christmas is demonstrated in how much we reach out beyond ourselves to help others and to express love, especially for those outside of our immediate families.

In the Bible, the Wise Men followed a star and when they reached the stable where Jesus lay, they humbly laid their gifts at his feet in a spirit of worship. Because they had been warned in a dream not to return to Herod, they went home by a different route. That decision demonstrates that <u>no</u> one ever travels the same path in the same way after coming to Jesus. Our routes and our lives are changed once we have found our own personal Bethlehem Once we have bowed down before the Master and surrendered our lives in service to Him, what does He do? He turns around and gives US gifts – the gifts of peace and eternal life!

When Christmas is over, let's put the <u>things</u> of Christmas away, but let's not put away the <u>theme</u> of Christmas, or the <u>message</u> of Christmas, or the <u>meaning</u> of Christmas. Let's do as Mary did – let's ponder these things and keep them in our hearts. With just a little effort, and the help of God, we can continue all through the year to be like ornaments of God as we reflect the beauty of His love, this precious holiday and the beautiful season.

Cynthia Irish Hockins

When they (the Magi) saw the star, they were overjoyed.
On coming to the house, they saw the child with his mother Mary,
and they bowed down and worshiped him. Then they opened
their treasures and presented him with gifts of
gold, and of incense and of myrrh.
Matthew 1:10, 11

Trees

———— § ————

TREES ARE USUALLY planted in the spring or summer when temperatures are pleasant. When a tree is planted, it signals new life and new growth. In preparation for the tree, the ground must be made ready to accept it. A large hole is dug and once the tree is set into its new location, earth is packed around it and the hole is now filled with earth to protect and encourage the root system. During this process it is important that the tree remain straight so it won't grow crooked or, worse yet, topple over before this new location accepts it. Sometimes it is even necessary to "stake" the tree with special supports, but most trees don't need that for long and they soon stand on their own.

Once this tree is in its new setting, it is extremely important that it be fed and watered regularly to assure that it will grow and thrive. Occasionally, the tree must be clipped or pruned so it can maintain its shape and grow even straighter and taller – and stronger.

So far, do you see where this process can be compared to our lives? We can easily equate this to a mother giving birth to a child. Once conception has taken place, the new mother must prepare herself mentally as well as physically to accept this new life. She must care for herself personally, physically, and emotionally as changes take place in her body and the child prepares to be born. Once the baby arrives, he or she must be fed regularly, both spiritually and emotionally. Also, as the child grows, he or she may require "clipping and pruning" in order to grow properly and become mature. By instilling Christian values and teaching the child about Jesus and His sacrifice for us, it is our sincere prayer that the child will stand straighter and taller, and be stronger against the winds of change and the inclement weather it will face now and then.

Think for a moment about the majestic redwood trees. You might think that anything of that stature would have extremely large, deep roots going down toward the center of the earth. In truth, despite their height and their breadth, they have a very shallow root system. What keeps them upright and helps them through wind and storms is the fact that their roots intertwine and in this way, they help each other! After reading about the redwood's root system, I read about the tumbleweed. It has no root system as such. Its roots are flimsy and so shallow that the tumbleweed is blown here and there. It has no particular direction. The tumbleweed needs deep roots in order to survive. Sometimes we may feel like a tumbleweed as the storms of life blow around us, but that's when we can hold still and lean on Jesus!

John Muir was a well-known early conservationist and naturalist in the west and he felt strongly about protecting and enjoying our God-given resources. Muir Woods, a beautiful redwood tree area in northern California, was named for him. My husband Dick and I visited there years ago and I don't think I have ever felt more insignificant than when I stood in the midst of those trees and read about their history at the park. At one time John Muir said this: *"Climb the mountains and get their good tidings. Nature's peace will flow into you as sunshine flows into trees. The winds and storms will blow their own freshness into you, and share their energy, while cares will drop off like autumn leaves."*

The strongest trees are not always in a forest being protected and held up by others. Many of the strongest are the ones standing by themselves in the open fields. They stand alone against the elements. They may be bent and misshapen by winds and storms of all seasons, but they are proud, and they thrive nonetheless!

Let's encourage our root systems to spread and deepen. Let's be nourished through God's Word and His beautiful promises so we may stand tall against the world and the devil through all the seasons of our lives. Let's strengthen ourselves with the love and Word of God. Then we can be content in the knowledge that we belong to Him as we each reach and grow, for now and for eternity!

> *Be still before the Lord and wait patiently for him.*
> *Psalm 37:7*

The C's of Christmas

—— ∮ ——

CHRISTMAS IS A time of the calendar year – it's a holiday – it's a time of <u>celebration</u> and often it is a time of families <u>coming</u> together. It is a time for <u>carols</u> and beautiful music. There are three other C's that further accent the true meaning of Christmas and Christendom.

The first C is the <u>crib</u>. The crib was in a small manger in a small town where the inn was full of travelers and had no room for more. Not even room for a pregnant woman and her husband who had traveled by donkey from Nazareth to Bethlehem so they could be counted as part of the census ordered by Caesar Augustus. Although the innkeeper in Bethlehem had no vacant rooms to offer, he did the best he could to help them when he offered Mary and Joseph his stable. Arriving at the stable outside of the inn they found a small manger and filled it with straw. After the birth of Jesus, it became his crib. That crib marked the end of Mary's pregnancy and the beginning of a new era.

The second C is a <u>crown</u>. Jesus, born humbly in that quiet, rural stable and without any fanfare, was later recognized by many as a Savior sent by God. After He began his ministry He was called the King of Kings and His kingly crown was the Holy Spirit in the form of an invisible protective halo that hovered over Him wherever He went. Near the end of His reign as King of Kings, He wore a different kind of crown. He was arrested in the Garden of Gethsemane and taken before Caiaphas and Pilate and other members of the Sanhedrin. He was accused of claiming to be the Son of God. He was found guilty and the soldiers molded a thorny branch into a circle and harshly pushed it down on His head as a makeshift crown. They did this to mock Him and all of His claims. He wore this crown as He trudged through the streets carrying the burden of this cross. This crown signaled the end of Jesus' life here on earth, but it also marked the beginning of a new era for Christians everywhere.

This brings us to the third C – that <u>cross</u> that Jesus carried. That cross was huge! It was also very heavy because it held all the sins of all mankind, but He bore it silently as He slowly moved His way through the city streets toward the hill outside of town called Golgotha, the Place of the Skull. It was here that large nails were pounded through His hands and His feet and the cross was then raised with the dying body of Jesus. That cross marked the ending of Jesus' ministry on earth, but it also marked a beginning as the number of His followers continued to spread and grow – and it is still spreading and growing today!

While Mary and Joseph were in Bethlehem, the time came for the
baby to be born, and Mary gave birth to her firstborn, a son.
She wrapped him in cloths and placed him in a manger,
because there was no room for them in the inn.
Luke 2:6-7

Arms

§

LORD, I SAW an artist's picture of You today. You were standing with Your head slightly bowed and Your arms were outstretched before You with Your palms up. What a beautiful way to picture you, dear Father – beckoning to us – urging us to come to You. I've seen other pictures of You with Your arms fully extended – as if to fold us in if we will but let You. I've also seen pictures of You reaching out to people – and gently touching people. All of these pictures depict You using Your arms almost like wings.

Seeing You like that makes me think of Your words in Luke, Father, where You speak of gathering Jerusalem protectively into Your arms as a hen gathers her brood under her wings. You are SO willing to reach out to me, Lord. Help me to be more willing to BE reached! Bring me ever closer into the protective circle of Your loving, outstretched arms.

The eternal God is your refuge,
and underneath are the everlasting arms.
Deuteronomy 33:27

Purpose

In Genesis, the very first book of The Bible, we are told that God created it all. In the beginning God created the heavens and the earth and then light and darkness – and land and seas. Then he went on to create vegetation and creatures and animals of all kinds, both wild and tame. Next he created man and woman. After each of these creative bursts, we read that *"God saw that it was good."* Each of his creations was done with a definite purpose – a reason. The dictionary says that the word purpose means what one plans to do. If something has a purpose, it is not accidental – it is intentional. It is done toward a specific end or goal – it is done deliberately. It all came about as the result of a plan. God had a plan – a purpose – and he fulfilled it intentionally and resolutely.

You can probably come up with a number of things that could be listed as having a purpose or a plan – or things that require a purpose or a plan. One thing I thought of is a blueprint. A blueprint shows the intricate and finite details of someone's intention to create something. In the case of a house or a building, for example, each part of the blueprint is important, and when the blueprints are drawn, down to the last and least detail, and then followed down to the last and least detail, the end result is a habitable house or building. These blueprints give you a good idea of what things will look like upon completion. There is always a Master Blueprint, of course, but then there are often separate blueprints for the carpenters and the electricians and the brick layers, etc. Each of these professions requires intricate details that all meld together in the end to bring a blueprint to life.

Let's think of God as our Master Architect. We, too, were created, right down to the last detail, - even to the number of hairs on our heads! – to fulfill God's purpose. God also created the Bible for us to use as OUR blueprint for living our lives. The Bible is our guide – our plan - our recipe for a life that He intended. A life that is to be filled with peace and joy - and all of it with the love of God in our hearts.

Creation, as laid out in the book of Genesis, was the fulfillment of God's plan for His world. We, as one of God's creations, are the result of His meticulous planning. Let's remember to thank Him for our lives – and for everything that He supplies according to our needs. Talk to God! Ask Him to show you your purpose for being. Ask Him to live in your heart and to direct your days and your ways. Remember - He is a God of details – and everything He does is done for – and with - a purpose.

And we know that in all things
God works for the good of those who love him,
who have been called according to His purpose.
Romans 8:28

Kites

THE DICTIONARY DESCRIBES a kite as a light wooden frame covered with paper or cloth, to be flown in the wind at the end of a string. It also states that the highest sails of a ship are called kites. This was a new definition to me, but it certainly makes good sense when you picture a ship gliding across the water in the wind with its sails billowing out.

I can remember trying to fly a kite many times when I was young. Word would spread quickly all around the neighborhood when the local drugstore received a supply of kites. All the kids hurried to get there to pick one out. Dad helped me put mine together in the right shape and then Mom helped me tear pieces of old fabric into strips to tie together to make a long tail. Dad whittled the ends down on a stick about 10" long and then he wound string onto it for me to hold onto after he attached it to the back of the kite where the 2 sticks of thin wood crossed. I remember my dad telling me that a kite cannot fly on its own. He told me to hold the stick tightly but to hold it at each end so the string could unwind easily as I loosened my grip ever so slightly and the kite rose slowly into the air. Then he told me to start running across the open field while letting the string out slowly. To a young child, that's a lot of instruction to absorb, but to achieve my goal I had to listen and pay attention and then I had to follow my Dad's instructions carefully.

As the kite rose in the air I learned how important the wind could be to my success or my failure. It could be my friend or my enemy. I also had to keep my eye on the kite as it rose and to the direction it was taking. Occasionally that meant changing my direction to go with the wind. I had to be aware of where I was running and of any tree branches and telephone lines around me so the kite wouldn't get caught and then come tumbling to the ground, usually in shreds. Kites were only made of very flimsy paper back then and they were not made to last long, but they could still bring kids a great deal of pleasure while they were able to fly. We almost felt like <u>we</u> were flying too!

Jesus could be said to be a little like a kite in our lives. Once we learn about Him and know He's there to help and guide us, we hurry toward Him and we go in his direction. Our parents and other adults surround us with their experiences and encourage us to tie all the areas of our lives together and to attach them to Jesus. They encourage us to follow His examples and to learn more about His teachings. Maybe we could say that God is a little like the string on the kite. He is really in control of the kite – or us - and He will let our string out a little at a time as we move ahead and catch the wind and move at His will. Our lives follow the wind's twists and turns, but if we always keep our eyes on God, we will be okay. We have to watch out for sin and the devil. They will try to ensnare us by catching us in branches and wires with temptations that are meant to make us stumble and fall, and to break our spirits. But, by keeping our eyes on God, we can soar and reach new heights in our eternal walk with our Lord and Savior. Each of us needs to remember where to focus and to concentrate on Jesus, His lessons and His words.

He who forms the mountains, creates the wind, and reveals
his thoughts to man, he who turns dawn to dark-
ness, and treads the high places
of the earth – the Lord God Almighty is his name.
Amos 4:13

Love

—— ∫ ——

Thoughts on love from things I've heard and read...

Love is God working in us.

In order to give love, you must experience it.

Love is friendship set to music.

Love starts when another person's needs become more important than your own.

Love is to be given, not measured.

The language of love is what you do. It needs no words.

Love does not dominate, it cultivates.

NAPOLEON ONCE SAID, "*Caesar, Charlemagne and I created great empires. Upon what did our genius depend? Upon force. But Jesus built His empire on love, and millions follow Him.*"

When the heart loves, the eyes talk.

Special verses on love...

I John 3:11   *This is the message we have heard from the beginning that we should love one another.*

I John 3:18   *Little Children, let us not love in word or speech, but in deed and truth.*

I John 4:7 — *Beloved, let us love one another, for love is of God.*

I Corinthians 8:1 — *"Knowledge" puffs up, but love builds up.*

John 14:15 — *If you love me you will keep my commandments.*

Proverbs 17:9 — *Love forgets mistakes.*

I Corinthians 13:13 — *So faith, hope, love abide, these three; but the greatest of these is love.*

Galatians 5:14 — *The entire law is summed up in a single command: "Love your neighbor as yourself."*

Family

§

THE WORD "FAMILY" isn't a very long word – only six letters linked together to form three syllables. The dictionary says a family is "all the people living in the same house" or "a social unit consisting of parents and their children" or "a group of people related by ancestry or marriage."

God thought a lot about families. He even chose to have his only Son born into a family. It wasn't a family of wealth or renown. It was not a majestic, royal group – it was a little-known carpenter and his lovely young bride in a small, out-of-the-way town out in the middle of nowhere.

By being a family Jesus could better identify with us and our daily lives. He had an earthly father and a Heavenly Father – just like you and I do. He was guided and led by his parents, as we were, and He also led his parents and He taught <u>them</u>, just as my children did when they were young, and they are still doing it today! (I learn from them all the time!)

Jesus loved and respected his earth family. Even as he hung on the cross, he turned to his beloved disciple John and asked him to take care of Mary, his mother. He wanted to be sure she would be looked after when he was no longer here in the flesh. Isn't that a beautiful picture of caring and love?

We have an earthly family we are responsible to, and we have the Triune family in heaven watching over and caring for us, Father, Son and Holy Spirit. We should remember to thank God regularly for this gift that we are privileged to enjoy here on earth, and also to thank him for the gift of His Son and the presence of the Holy Spirit that assure us an eventual place in our Heavenly home!

> *So God created man in his own image, in the image of God*
> *he created him; male and female he created them.*
> *Genesis 1:27*

Garden

---§---

GOD IS LIKE a Master Gardener and our lives are a garden. He sows us in sunshine (Sonshine) and gives us the nourishment we need to grow. He waters us with the dew and rains of life. The rain sometimes comes in a gentle sprinkle, but occasionally it comes as a stormy torrent. Often God sees a need for us to be pruned and cut back. Although painful at the time, this helps us to flourish and to grow better, more satisfying fruit. It can help us lead fuller, more productive lives. Although weeds may spread and try to edge us out, God, our unseen Gardener, comes along and uproots them and removes their thorns. When Satan moves in, in the form of bugs and insects, God's strength is there to help us fend them off.

Like the Raid commercials years ago, as soon as sin sees His great shadow towering overhead, it crumbles and runs away. We should be certain our garden is planted in Grace. We must keep the sky clear overhead and let the dew of heaven in daily and bask in the sunshine of His love so we drink in the waters of His goodness. We must keep our faces upturned to Him as flowers to the sun. Self must step aside and let God do the work. When a seed is planted in the ground, it dies – and from it comes the shoot above the ground. Jesus was a seed – the Seed of Christianity. After being buried in the ground, He arose and grew and His word spread and we reap the benefits!

In I Corinthians Paul said his work was to plant the seed in our hearts, his helper was Apollos and his job was to water the seed and keep it refreshed, but it is God who makes the garden grow. In verse 7 he goes on to say the one who plants and the one who waters are not as important as God because He is the only one who can truly make things grow.

The strength exerted by a seedling as it pushes its stem above the ground's surface is roughly 450 pounds per square inch! If He has given an organism smaller than the size of my fingernail such strength, how much must I have inside me, yet untapped?

A man once acquired a rundown piece of land and made it into a beautiful garden. A friend remarked, "Isn't it wonderful what God can do with worn out soil?" The owner replied, "You should have seen this plot when God was taking care of it by Himself!" That is the way God wants it – He provides us with the means, the strength, the intelligence to produce "crops" – He does not <u>do</u> our gardening. He wants <u>us</u> to do the work!

Ask yourself, "Am I a bush or a tree?" A tree stands tall against the storms of life. A tree is firmly rooted in the deep awareness of God and can be a shelter for others. Its roots go deep enough to touch an underground stream of Living Water so that a dry spell leaves it calm and unscathed. On the other hand, a bush, or shrub, often has very <u>shallow</u> roots. When there is a dry spell it cowers and withers and begins to droop and shrivel. It cannot help itself let alone help anyone else.

Remember that he who sows in hope will reap in <u>joy</u>! Pray for forgiveness and for His power so you sow in the Spirit and the harvest of the Spirit is everlasting life!

The righteous will flourish like a palm tree, they
will grow like a cedar of Lebanon;
planted in the house of the Lord, they will flour-
ish in the courts of our God.
Psalm 92:12

Hope

THE DICTIONARY DEFINES hope as a feeling that what is wanted will happen. Hope is an inward feeling – a wish – a desire that things will go as planned. A Bible Concordance defines hope as a reliance on God's blessing and provision – the expectation of future good.

Abraham was an excellent example of hope. He listened – well, most of the time. He followed, he confessed, he prayed, he believed, and all because God was his hope and because God was the center of his life.

The writer of Hebrews says that our hope is certain. It is an anchor for our soul to hold onto. In Romans 12 we are admonished to rejoice in hope and to be patient in suffering and to persevere in prayer.

In Romans Chapter 5 there is another reference to hope. Years ago, during my husband's annual physical, the doctor noticed what he thought could become a serious problem and he ordered a special stress test for Dick at a large hospital in Indianapolis. I went with him and as I waited in the waiting room I had my Bible Study lesson with me and the main verses that morning were these in Romans Chapter 5: *"We rejoice in our sufferings, because we know that suffering produces perseverance, perseverance produces character, and character produces hope – and hope does not disappoint us, because God has poured out his love into our hearts by the Holy Spirit, whom he has given us."* That day I took those verses to heart in a positive way, and Dick's test was fine. Early the following year my 9th grade daughter required surgery on her hand after several months of therapy. Although nothing was broken, she had injured ligaments and tendons in an accident while cheerleading. She was also a piano player and we were afraid of long-term problems that might complicate her playing. I kissed her goodbye as they wheeled her off to surgery and settled down with a daily devotional book, and there were these exact same verses from Romans 5. I thanked God for his assurances that Dick's test and Linda's surgery would only make them stronger – and better – and I thanked him for easing my concerns and replacing them with these positive words.

The Psalmist says, *"Happy are those whose help is the God of Jacob, whose hope is in the Lord their God."* He also said, *"For you, O Lord, are my hope, you are my trust, O Lord, from my youth,"* in Psalm 71, and in Psalm 39 David said, *"My hope is in thee."*

A writer once said we should never deprive someone of hope because it may be all they have! We should encourage hope in others and use it as something to hold onto for ourselves. When we think of hope, let's think of it as putting a smile on our faces as we go forward with patience, courage, and confidence. Remember, we should look to the Lord to be the source of our hope. As we continue to put our hope and our trust in Him, let us also remember to thank him for this gift of hope.

"May the God of hope fill you with all joy and peace today and always so that you may abound in hope by the power of the Holy Spirit."
Romans 15:13

Lydia

§

(A story from Paul's 2ⁿᵈ Missionary Journey - Acts 16:14)

THIS IS THE story of Lydia, a woman in the Bible who was in the right place, at the right time, with the right heart, and the right attitude. Scripture does not give us much information regarding Lydia's background other than the fact that she was a prominent woman in Thyatira, one of the Macedonian colonies, and also in Philippi which was considered a melting pot of many nations. The chief object of worship here was Apollo, who was worshiped as the sun-god. Lydia's faith and conversion were brought about through hearing the Word of God. She is only mentioned in a few Bible verses but the fact that she was mentioned at all makes her important.

While visiting Philippi on his travels, Paul went outside the city gate to the river where he planned to find a place to pray. There were several women gathered there and Paul began to speak to them. One who was listening was Lydia. The Lord opened her heart to hear and respond to Paul's message and after listening to Paul and his message, she asked that she and the members of her household be baptized. This implies that she was probably wealthy because she had a home, and she had servants and/or relatives living with her. Lydia's transformation, followed by her baptism was evident by her eagerness to give these missionaries the hospitality of her fine home. She invited Paul and Silas to stay there, and they did. You might say the Holy Spirit led Paul to her because God knew her heart was right for this experience. While the missionaries benefitted from Lydia's generous hospitality, Paul warned all of those present of the terrible trials that lay before them as Christians, and later, when parting from this godly Lydia, he praised God for all she had meant to him and his companions.

Lydia was not only very hospitable, she was also a conscientious business woman and a "seller of purple." Purple was the name for a dye which was made from shellfish found in and around Thyatira. The fluid from these special shellfish was placed on wool, which turned the wool blue. Then it was exposed to the sunlight, which turned it green, and finally it turned purple. And then, when it was washed in water it became a brilliant crimson-red. This was not only widely desired, it also brought a high price. Purple cloth was considered to be valuable and it was very expensive. It was mainly worn by princes and by the rich as a sign of nobility or royalty, so making and selling it would be very profitable. The dye was claimed to be worth its weight in silver. This gives new significance to the passage in Mark 15:17 where it says the soldiers put a purple robe on Jesus, then twisted together a crown of thorns and set it on him. And they began to call out to him, "hail, king of the Jews!" Lydia not only sold her dyes and purple cloth – she continued to serve her Savior. She used her money to help God's servants in their ministry.

In closing, when we reach heaven, we shall find this "seller of purple" and she will be wearing superior garments – robes not stained with the notable dye of Thyatira, but clothing "washed and made white in the blood of the Lamb."

"When she and the members of her household
were baptized, she invited us to her home.
'If you consider me a believer in the Lord,' she said,
'come and stay at my house.'"
Acts 16:15

Availability

THE MOST IMPORTANT ability we have is our <u>avail</u>ability. Of all the many gifts from God, this is one gift He likes to see multiplied and growing. He wants us to be ready and able to serve Him whenever opportunities present themselves. The main thing that matters is how we respond to God's gifts and also the challenges He puts before us.

We are each given many different varieties of talents and skills, often far more than we can fully develop. He does not want us to be content with a small garden in a large field. He wants us to encourage growth in our gardens so these gardens will reach out and spread. This type of attention to detail will further help us to expand and develop our aptitudes and our attitudes to the best of our ability as new opportunities present themselves. Then we are to apply this knowledge, not just to our own satisfaction, but also to His satisfaction.

Remember, it's not the number or size of the abilities and opportunities God gives each of us that counts. It is what we choose to do with them and how we utilize and share them that pleases God. Even those who feel their talents are small should acknowledge them gratefully and use them to the best of their ability. We should also use these talents thankfully and graciously, because each is a God-given gift.

As you know, we consider blessed those who have persevered.
You have heard of Job's perseverance and have seen what the Lord
finally brought about. The Lord is full of compassion and mercy.
James 5:11

Busy, Busy

—◊—

Oh, Lord,

I really need you today! All those things written down on my calendar – and the timings on some are going to be pretty close! Help me as I go about my list that I can sort out the necessary from the unnecessary. Help me keep my mind on what I am doing at the moment – don't let me be overly concerned about later until later.

I'm so glad every day isn't like this one, Lord. Now I will appreciate tomorrow because I won't have so much to do – but wait! Look at tomorrow! Oh, how did I let that happen? There's the early meeting, cleaning to be picked up, basketball practice after school, and the orthodontist appointment. We need to have an early dinner, too, because of the meeting afterward.

Well, the NEXT day I can relax a little. Then I can put my feet up and get back to my needlework project - just as soon as I get the birthday cake baked and the dessert dishes out, and pick up the kids for piano lessons....

Be very careful, then, how you live –
not as unwise, but as wise, making the most
of every opportunity, because the days are evil.
Ephesians 5:15-16

She watches over the ways of her household......
Proverbs 31:27

Architect

§

AN ARCHITECT IS one who designs plans for a building. He can also be a carpenter, a designer, or a planner. Stop for a moment, and think of God in the role of an architect. He was indeed a Master Planner. We could also call Him the Supreme Architect because He planned and designed our world and all that is in it, and then He created each of us. God is truly an architect, and one with a vision!

In Genesis we are told how God created and formed the earth. Then He created and formed the plants and animals, followed by the humans, male and female, who would inhabit and care for the world He created. Later, meticulous instructions were given to Noah when it was time to build the ark. He was told what materials would be required and He had very specific instructions about the building of something of this enormous size.

In Exodus our Supreme Architect told Moses to have the people make a sanctuary for Him and He told Moses how to build it and how to make its furnishings. Again, God showed Himself as an Architect – one with a plan and a pattern. Later he went on to tell Moses that a few chosen men would be instructed on how to do the work of craftsmen, designers, weavers, etc., to create the beautiful furnishings for this tabernacle. God told them they would become master craftsmen with His help.

In I Chronicles we are told that David shared the plans for the portico of the temple with his son Solomon. These plans, which had been given to David by God, included the buildings, storerooms, upper parts, inner rooms, and the place of atonement. God had even specified the weight of the gold and the silver to be used for each item in the temple. After sharing these instructions with Solomon, David urged Solomon to be strong and courageous as he did this work.

The dictionary says that before something can be constructed it must have an appropriate base to support it. New buildings often have a cornerstone which is laid to announce new construction. An archway or doorway may have a capstone at its center. Matthew, Mark and John all make reference to Jesus as the "stone the builders rejected" because He was disdained by the rulers and worldly powers of that time, but He became the most important "stone" in the structure of the new world order that God was bringing about. Jesus applied this verse to Himself in these Gospels. Today we can refer to Jesus as our cornerstone because He is the foundation and the capstone and the cornerstone upon which we build our lives!

When the builders laid the foundation of the temple of the Lord,
the priests in their vestments and with trum-
pets, and the Levites, with cymbals,
took their places to praise the Lord, as pre-
scribed by David King of Israel.
Ezra 3:10

Humility

———— § ————

ACCORDING TO WEBSTER'S Dictionary, humility is the act of being humble, to be unpretentious, to be unassuming, to be modest. A Bible Concordance describes humility as "the recognition of one's true position before God." Jesus, Peter and Paul each have something to say about humility.

Jesus speaks in Luke 14 saying that everyone who tries to honor himself shall be humbled; and he who humbles himself shall be honored. Later, in Luke 18:14, the Living Bible tells us that Jesus said the proud shall be humbled but the humble shall be honored. Later, in I Peter 5:5 Peter tells us to be submissive to those who are older and to clothe ourselves with humility toward one another because God opposes the proud but gives grace to the humble.

In Ephesians 4:1-4, Paul asks us to live a life worthy of the calling we have received as Christians. He says we are to be completely humble and gentle; to be patient, bearing with one another in love. He adds that we are to make every effort to keep the unity of the Spirit through the bond of peace. In verse 5 he concludes that we have one Lord, one faith, one baptism – one Father of us all. In the book of Colossians, Paul says that as Christians we are advised to clothe ourselves with compassion, kindness, humility, gentleness and patience. Elsewhere in Philippians Paul again says that we are to be humble. He challenges us not to just think of our own affairs but be interested in others, too, and in what they are doing. He reminds us that Jesus humbled himself by suffering the humiliation of death on the cross.

Someone once said that humility is silence before God. Humility means we are smart enough to know we cannot know everything. Humility is thankful for all it has, and because it has received so much, it also gives unendingly. Humility opens the way to God and happiness. One is often tempted to talk humility --- and it is easy to find plenty of opportunities to do so – but it is far better to be humbly silent. Talkative humility tends to appear pretentious and it can make those around us become suspicious. Truly, nothing is more humbling than to open one's heart and lay bare all of one's weaknesses, and yet nothing draws a better blessing!

In the Old Testament, God describes Moses as a very humble man – more humble than anyone else on the face of the earth at that time. That was a beautiful compliment to Moses. Humility is subtle. The moment you think you have it, you have lost it! You cannot strive for humility. It comes by learning to be submissive and by giving of yourself to help others.

If humility and obedience had NOT been important to Jesus, Paul tells us there would be no forgiveness, no salvation, and no heaven. He urges us to be humble enough to serve others, as Jesus would have, and then to be quiet about it. Let's remember, true humility is smart enough to know we cannot know everything. True humility is thankful for all it has, and because it has received so much, it gives unendingly because it wants to give! This kind of true humility opens our communications with God, improves our relationship with God, and it leads to greater happiness. Forget your own self-importance and focus on the needs of others in an attitude of humility.

Humble yourselves before the Lord, and he will lift you up. James 4:10

God's Gifts to Us

———— § ————

Air we breathe
Bible for guidance and reassurance
Conscience
Daylight
Encouragement
Forgiveness
Grace
Heaven (eventually)
Independence
Joy
Knowledge
Life and Life Eternal
Mercy
Nourishment through His words
Opportunities
Patience
Quiet
Rest & Rejuvenation
Seasons – Sun – Stars – His Son
Talents
Universe
Values
Wisdom
Youth
Zest for life

Touch

————— ∫ —————

THE DICTIONARY GIVES many definitions of the word touch. These definitions include: to feel, to bring into contact with, to affect by contact, to arouse an emotion as in gratitude or in sympathy. My Bible Concordance explains it as making physical contact with something, especially with one's hands. It then goes on to list about 75 verses in the Old Testament and almost 50 verses in the New Testament that make a reference to some kind of touching.

When we touch velvet we think of something soft and smooth. When we touch tissue paper we notice how thin and delicate it is compared to a paper bag that is tough and can take rough handling. When we touch sand-paper it feels harsh and grating.

Now let's think of the touch of Jesus. Jesus touched a leper and was rebuked for touching something so unclean, but the leper was healed. Jesus touched water at the wedding in Cana and it turned into wine. Jesus touched a blind man's eyes and those eyes were opened and able to see. Jesus touched many human lives and those lives were changed forever. Saul became Paul; Simon became Peter, the Rock; Jacob became Israel; Sarah became a mother; a woman of affliction touched Jesus' garment and was healed. Her touch was different from other touches by the crowds and Jesus was immediately sensitive to her needs. These are only a few examples of His touch and its effect on people in Biblical times.

The touch of Jesus today can offer new courage – or a new beginning. It can instill confidence. It can be soft as in a caress, but at times it can seem harsh as it seeks to correct, but it is always tender and loving.

Jesus touched words like grace, and sacrifice, and love, and mercy and these words became even more beautiful and meaningful. When He touches our lives He can calm our fears and then dry our tears.

We can all benefit from human touch. We are never too old or too young for a loving touch or a hug. We all know that a baby thrives and benefits from being touched and cuddled, and so does an older person. Personally, I think there's nothing nicer than a friendly pat on the shoulder, or a good, loving hug now and then!

"And He took the children in his arms,
put his hands on them and blessed them."
Mark 10:16

Sonshine

Oh, Lord,

It's so cloudy and "blah" outside today. Why do you suppose I think more about You on a cloudy day? Maybe it's because I want some brightness around me – and if I can't have sunshine, I'll look for Sonshine!

There are so many ways You brighten my life every day, Lord! Forgive me for not always remembering to say thanks as often as I should.

You talk a lot about light in Your Words in the Bible, Lord. You speak of light around us and about us being a light for others. Light can also be cleansing.

I don't want to grope and stumble in the dark because I might latch onto Satan's coattails instead of Your glorious Robe of Righteousness. If I don't ask for Your light around me, I could miss something truly good you are planning for my life!

Remind me to shine Your light today, Father. Let me bask in Your light and let me be some kind of a beacon to someone who may be in danger, just like a lighthouse beacon warns the sailors of the rocky coasts.

Abundant Sonshine

For it is the God who commanded light to shine out of darkness
who has shone in our hearts to give the light of the knowledge
of the glory of God in the face of Jesus Christ.
II Corinthians 4:6

Heart

IN THE BOOK of Ephesians Jesus tells us to open the eyes of our heart. Only eyes of the heart can see love, experience joy, and sense mystery. It is not always easy to focus those inner eyes, but as they develop through meditation and prayerful submission, they unveil a new and marvelous world.

There is approximately 12 inches between your head (or your brain) and your heart. Don't let a foot get in your way and separate you from the love of Christ! You need not only head-knowledge but also a heart-relationship too.

Our hearts beat 103,689 times in 24 hours; our blood travels 168 million miles. We breathe 23,040 times, inhaling 438 cubic feet of air, moving 750 muscles, and exercising 7 million brain cells. Let's thank God for our bodies and how they function!

A writer once said we should ask ourselves if our heart is in "stable condition." The stable was unsuitable for the birth of a king, because it offered no comforts, but it did offer room, and that is what the inn lacked. Is my heart like that inn? Is it so crowded that I am missing the sweet presence of the Son of God? Am I so filled with cares there is no room left for Jesus?" In remembering this Christmas story about the inn my thoughts turn to the innkeeper. He did the best he could with what he had to offer by sending them to the stable.

Each day I have opportunities to allow God's blessings and power to fill my heart. When I have meditated and communicated with him through prayer, my day unfolds and I am better able to handle situations with wisdom and strength from Him.

Helen Keller said it best when she said, *"The best and most beautiful things in the world cannot be seen or even touched. They must be felt with the heart."*

Therefore my heart is glad and my tongue rejoices;
my body also will live in hope, because you will not
abandon me to the grave, nor will you let your Holy One see decay.
Acts 2:26

Borrowed

WHEN ALL THE prophets of the Old Testament were predicting the coming of a Savior, the Messiah, He was often spoken of as a King and references were made to His Kingdom. Because of that, the people naturally expected Jesus to be of a royal lineage. What a shock it must have been when they realized He was born of "average" parents in the small town of Bethlehem – and not in a palace, as the son of a king or queen. He was not only born in a stable, but in a borrowed stable at that!

Late in His ministry when Jesus told His disciples of His impending death, He rode into Jerusalem on a borrowed donkey, and the people honored Him by waving palm branches and then laying them at His feet. They must have known He was not "royalty," but He was still a king in their eyes! They realized He was "special."

After Jesus was crucified, His friends took His body from the cross and anointed Him, and then they buried Him in a borrowed tomb. The tomb belonged to a rich man named Joseph of Arimathea. but Jesus Himself had not been rich by those same standards.

Following the resurrection of Jesus, He talked with His disciples and they went out in a borrowed boat and spent time together near the shore – alone and quiet. Time alone and away from crowds was always important to Jesus throughout His ministry. He used that time to pray as well as to rest and prepare Himself for what lay ahead.

What an enigma He was to the people of His day. A Savior and King, born in a <u>borrowed stable</u>, riding on a <u>borrowed donkey</u>, buried in a <u>borrowed tomb</u>, and later setting out in a <u>borrowed boat</u>! This was proof that His kingdom was not of this earth, but that His is a *heavenly* kingdom! We will have the opportunity to know this kingdom some day if we accept Him as our Savior and the Lord of our lives. Then we can be part of eternity with Him and we can also have eternal life! And all because He was NOT too proud to be a borrower!

Finally, brothers, whatever is true, whatever is noble, whatever is right,
whatever is pure, whatever is lovely, whatever is admirable –
if anything is excellent or praiseworthy – think about such things.
Whatever you have learned or received or heard from me, or seen in me,
put it into practice. And the God of peace will be with you.
Philippians 4:8,9

Names for Jesus
in the Bible

—— ♪ ——

Branch	Isaiah 11:1
Creator	Psalm 146:6
Emancipator	Psalm 146:7
Everlasting Father	Isaiah 9:6
Healer	Psalm 146:8
Holy One of Israel	Isaiah 43:3
Holy Servant	Acts 4:27
Immanuel	Isaiah 7:14
Lord Almighty	Isaiah 51:15
Man of Sorrows	Isaiah 53:3
Master (by a Scribe)	Matthew 8:19
Messenger	Malachi 3:1
Mighty God	Isaiah 9:6
Prince of Peace	Isaiah 9:6 & Zechariah 9:10
Prophet	Deuteronomy 18:18
Provider	Psalm 146:7
Ruler	Psalm 146:10
Savior	Isaiah 45:21
Son of God	Matthew 27:54
Star	Numbers 24:17
Teacher (by Nicodemus)	John 3:2
Wonderful Counselor	Isaiah 9:6

Shelter

———— ∮ ————

THE DICTIONARY SAYS a shelter is something that protects us from the elements or from danger. To provide shelter is to cover and to protect. This same dictionary describes a shield as something worn on the body to ward off blows; something that defends or protects.

I have always liked the image of Jesus being my shelter, my shield and my protector. He constantly keeps me from harm and danger by spreading his protective wings to cover me, much as a hen or mother bird would do for her young. Yet, that same protective mother bird will push her young ones OUT of the nest when the time is right. She hovers over them and feeds them, but eventually she knows it is time to let them go. She never totally abandons them, but she helps them learn to fly and she encourages their independence because if she doesn't, the birds might never be able to fend for themselves or defend themselves against predators. That mother bird realizes that her young must <u>develop</u> this confidence – it is not inborn. But then, neither are our faith and our confidence in the Lord! They, too, must be developed and cultivated -- and then we must be nourished regularly from that point forward. If we were not pushed "out of our nest," so to speak, we would never develop the spiritual strength we need to handle the upsets and storms as they swirl around us and come into our lives.

There are numerous references throughout the Bible showing Jesus as our shelter and our shield. Here are a few:

(1) God mentioned the shield in Genesis 15:1 as he spoke to Abram and told him, *"I am your shield."* He was reassuring Abram when he said this. Even though Abram was quite wealthy, Abram knew God himself was his greatest treasure. Abram was truly rewarded because today he is often referred to as "the father of all who believe."

(2) In Psalm 3 David says: *"But thou, O Lord, art a shield about me."* He will provide it, but we must request it. He knows our needs, but he wants us to express them and verbalize them. David makes references in this Psalm, and in many others, to the Lord assuring him of his waking and also "keeping" him while he sleeps. This tells us God is always faithful in his care and He sustains the Godly day <u>and</u> night, whatever the need or the circumstance. We know from David's writings that he had many enemies, but he knew he was chosen by God and he knew God was with him. More importantly, he knew God as a refuge, as a shelter, and as a shield.

(3) In Psalm 17 David asks God to keep him as the apple of his eye – and to hide him in the shadow of his wings. He's been dealing with his enemies and he needs to rest and recoup. This comes up again in Psalm 57:1 when David says *"for my soul trusts in You; in the shadow of Your wings I will make my refuge until these calamities have passed."*

(4) In Psalm 18 David is thanking God for his blessings and for helping him thrive among his enemies. David says the way of the Lord is perfect and His Word is flawless. He thanks God for being a shield for all who take refuge in Him and who feel His strength.

(5) Isaiah 43:2 says, *"When you pass through the waters, I will be with you; and through the rivers, they shall not overflow you."*

(6) In Psalm 91 David says *"He will cover you with his pinions, and under His wings you will find refuge; his faithfulness is a shield and buckler."*

(7) Along with all of David's references to shield and shelter thus far, again in Psalm 25 He asks the Lord to assign Godliness and integrity as body guards. Add these to God's shield and armor and we cannot

lose! With such formidable guards, who wouldn't feel special and important, and well protected!

We were never promised that our lives would be "fair" – or that we would have smooth-sailing – or that we would always have our own way – or that our lives would be without troubles or complications. We were not promised total sunshine for all our days. What we <u>were</u> promised is we never have to face our trials or problems alone. He will always be our shield – our shelter and our buffer. He promised us His continuing presence and also His unfailing devotion to us if we will just remember that He is there for us if we call on Him.

A man named Vernon Charlesworth, who was born in 1838, wrote a hymn in the 19th century about Jesus being *"A Shelter in the Time of Storm."* He was an English pastor who also served as headmaster of Charles Spurgeon's *Stockwell Orphanage.* An American gospel musician named Ira D. Sankey later added the melody and refrain. The wording in the hymn assures us we are safer during life's storms <u>with</u> Christ in control than in the calm times with<u>out</u> him. It's been said that this hymn is a favorite among fishermen on the northern coast of England because of the sudden storms that can develop so quickly in that area. They have been heard singing this hymn as they approach their harbors returning home from their fishing expeditions. The words go like this:

The Lord's our Rock – in Him we hide – secure whatever ill betide.
A shade by day, defense by night – no fears alarm, no foes affright.
The raging storms may round us beat – we'll never leave our safe retreat.
O Rock divine, O Refuge dear – be Thou our helper, ever
near.
Chorus: O Jesus is a Rock in a weary land, a weary land, a weary land;
O Jesus is a Rock in a weary land – a shelter in the time of storm.

Let's remember to thank God for the storms in our lives that have helped us develop a more spiritual strength. Then let's try to encourage someone around us who may currently be floundering in a difficult situation and be in need of the sheltering only He can give.

God is our refuge and strength, an ever present help in trouble.
Psalm 46:1

God's Promises

―――――― ◊ ――――――

The Lord did not promise life's path would be straight.
Rough hills and deep valleys lead up to His Gate.
Flat tires and detours could lead us astray.
But we must not falter as we make our way.

He gave us His Son as our armor and shield.
The sword of His Word will make enemies yield.
He promised His presence and light for our way.

He'll love us and lead us, forget and forgive
If only we follow then with Him we'll live.

No Mail Today

Hello Dear Lord,

The mail just came. No letters today. That makes me sad, Lord, but maybe You are telling me something on days like today. Maybe You are encouraging me to think of someone else – someone who just might need to have a letter in their box from me. Maybe with just a little effort, I can put some thoughts onto paper and wing them on their way to let someone know they are thought about and loved.

Receiving mail can bring love, but help me to remember that sending mail shows love too!

Guide my pen and my thoughts. Help me brighten someone else's day – and then perhaps tomorrow, someone else will brighten mine!

Like the coolness of snow at harvest is a trustworthy messenger
to those who send him; he refreshes the spirit of his masters.
Proverbs 25:13

Three

―――――――――― § ――――――――――

Have you noticed the repetitious use of certain numbers in the Bible? Think about some of the times the number three is mentioned in both the Old Testament and the New Testament.

After the parting of the Red Sea in Exodus 15, Moses and the Israelites wandered in the wilderness of the Desert of Shur for three days looking for water and they found none until they got to Marah. They moved on and God soon saw to their needs by giving them fresh Manna and quail each morning.

In Exodus 23, God told the people through Moses that they were to observe three annual festivals: (1) The Feast of Unleavened Bread, (2) The Feast of Harvest, and (3) The Feast of Ingathering. The first one meant eating bread made without yeast for about seven days between mid-March and mid-April. The second one was to be observed about seven weeks after the Feast of Unleavened Bread, usually about mid-May to mid-June. The third one was generally celebrated from mid-September to mid-October when the produce of the orchards and vines had been harvested. It commemorated the desert wanderings after the exodus.

In I Kings 17, Elijah stretched himself on top of the widow's dead son three times and cried to the Lord for the boy's spirit to return to him. The Lord heard Elijah's cries and the boy's life returned to him. The widow recognized Elijah as a true man of God because of this miracle.

We are told that Jonah was in the whale's belly for three days and nights and later, it took Jonah three days to walk to Nineveh where he accomplished what God sent him to do.

In the New Testament, in Jesus' younger days, he was missing from his parents for three days before he was found in the Temple courts among the teachers in Luke 2. Satan tempted Jesus three times in Matthew chapter 4. There were three mountains important in the life of Christ. The Sermon on the Mount in Matthew, chapter 5 where he gave us the Beatitudes; His Transfiguration with three of his disciples in attendance - Peter, James and John; and Calvary where He gave Himself up to his Father for us. Jesus blessed bread and broke it three different times – first at the feeding of the 5000, next at the feeding of the 4000, and again at the Last Supper before his arrest.

Later Jesus took three disciples, Peter, James & John, to the Garden of Gethsemane to keep watch so he could pray three prayers to His Father. Three times Jesus found all three disciples asleep as he prayed – and these same three watched as Jesus was arrested there in the Garden. Peter denied Jesus three times before he was crucified. Jesus was pierced three times – by the thorns in the Crown of Thorns, by the nails on the cross, and by the soldier's spear into his side as He was dying.

Jesus raised three people from the dead in the New Testament: Jabirus' daughter in Matthew, the widow's only son in Luke and Lazarus in John.

Jesus was in the tomb for three days and nights before the stone was rolled away and he arose from the dead.

After Jesus' resurrection John tells us that Jesus sat at the side of a lake with his disciples. He asked Peter three times, "Do you love me?" Each time Peter replied, "Yes, Lord." Jesus followed each reply with a challenge to feed

His lambs, take care of His sheep, and feed His sheep. It was like Jesus forgave Peter for each of his denials and He told him how to atone for each denial.

Paul was blinded three days after his conversion on the road to Damascus. Later he was beaten three times, shipwrecked three times, and he went on three missionary journeys.

You might say I've saved the best for last, because now we come to the Trinity – The Father, The Son, and The Holy Spirit. All three are referred to in the 1st chapter of the 1st book of the Bible, and all three are referred to in the last chapter of the last book of the Bible. Singly, and together, they are spoken of throughout the Bible. Today, we have the wonderful advantage of being able to have a personal contact and a personal relationship with each part of the Trinity, and we know in our hearts that the three are one in the same. God wants what is best for us, Jesus loved us enough to die for us, and the Spirit descended onto and into us at Pentecost to strengthen and preserve us in the image of God Himself. When we pray, let's pray in the name of the Father, the Son, and the Holy Spirit – the Trinity! How blessed we are to have this gift!

"The Lord said to Moses, 'Tell Aaron and his sons to bless
the Israelites. Say to them: 'The Lord bless you and keep you;
the Lord make his face shine upon you and be gracious to you;
the Lord turn his face toward you and give you peace.'"
Numbers 6:22-26

10 Facts Forty

THE BIBLE IS filled with things that have to do with the number forty. Here are just a few:

1. The flood in Genesis lasted forty days and after that, a new era began.
2. Moses was forty years old when he was exiled from Egypt by Pharaoh, and he was exiled for forty years.
3. Moses and the Israelites had manna daily for forty years until they arrived in Canaan.
4. Moses was on Mt. Sinai forty days and nights with the Lord.
5. The Israelites were in the desert for forty years.
6. Jonah warned Nineveh it would be destroyed in forty days.
7. King David reigned for forty years.
8. King Solomon reigned for forty years.
9. Jesus fasted forty days and nights and then he was tempted by the devil for forty days in the wilderness.
10. Jesus Christ appeared on earth to men for forty days after his resurrection, and again, a new era began.

Meekness

————— ◊ —————

AT ONE TIME I thought it was not a compliment to be called meek. I felt it meant you were timid or afraid, almost cowering. Then someone straightened me out by saying that meekness is not a form of weakness – it is an admirable trait – and one we should seek. This person went on to say it is a form of power under control. It is definitely a positive quality and one to be admired and sought after because it implies inner serenity and a humble belief in oneself.

Psalm 37:11 says, *"The meek shall possess the land, and delight themselves in abundant prosperity."* The Living Bible says, *"The meek shall be given every blessing and shall have wonderful peace."* Jesus spoke of meekness in the Beatitudes when he said, *"Blessed are the meek for they will inherit the earth."* The dictionary describes the word meek as being patient or mild; not inclined to anger or resentment. Roget's Thesaurus adds these words: gentle, tolerant, long-suffering, unresisting, unoffended, and tame. A Bible Concordance says it means patient or steadfast; not harboring resentment. Please note that the dictionary, the Thesaurus and the Bible Concordance do not refer to it as meaning a weakness. On the contrary, meekness is power under control. The meek person is not timid or shy because meekness is a positive quality – again, a kind of inner serenity.

A writer once wrote this about meekness: *"It is the meek who have learned to take time to enjoy the flowers that grow alongside the path."* He goes on to say, *"The meek individual is the one who gets God's work done in the world without a lot of showmanship or weird tactics."* You could say the meek man is disciplined. He is trained to take on great responsibilities and to discharge them without fuss or fanfare.

The Greek word for meek is *praus*. When used to describe sound, it means soft and gentle. When used to describe an animal it means a wild animal that has been tamed – one no less strong, but one whose strength has been channeled and made usable. When the word *praus* is used to describe a human being, it refers to a person who has been gentled and quieted, particularly after anger. This is not a weak person. This is a strong, spirited individual who has been tamed, or molded, by God. This form of meekness implies strength – a gentle power. It builds, it lifts up, and it restores.

The meek are the submitted ones. They have surrendered their human wills to God so that HE can use them as instruments of His power on this earth. Another writer said she liked to stretch the meaning to include being adaptable. Happy are the adaptable. She went on to say that when her own inner needs have been met, she finds she is much more adaptable to the needs of the people around her. So, in taming us, God makes us useful to the others we contact in our lives. This kind of meekness creates a pure inner joy that spreads and radiates through us to those around us.

So – today, let's strive to be called meek! Let's strive to have that inner joy that accompanies it and makes it all the more appealing and satisfying.

The Spirit of the Sovereign Lord is on me, because the Lord
has anointed me to preach good news to the poor.
Isaiah 61:1

Reason

---§---

"Jesus is the reason for the season." We hear that phrase constantly throughout the Christmas holidays and it certainly is a good reminder for us. All the glitz and the gifts, Santa Claus, Rudolph and Frosty the Snowman add a certain dimension to the holidays at this time of year, mainly for the youngsters, but we would all do well to focus more on the true reason we celebrate.

Jesus is also the reason John the Baptist was sent ahead to begin baptizing believers with water and to tell them to watch for the One who was coming soon who would baptize with the Spirit. He was to let the people know he had been sent by God – and also to let them know he was just a forerunner of the wondrous things that lay ahead for all of them.

Yes, Jesus is the reason for the season of Christmas – and for the ministry of John the Baptist -- but then Jesus is also the reason for the season of Easter. In the Bible we read of all the turmoil created by His presence and accusations of His strange sounding promises, and then we read of His arrest and trial – and His eventual conviction by unbelievers, and His crucifixion and death on the cross between two thieves. But then, wondrously, we also read of His resurrection! We hear how the stone was miraculously rolled away and angels announced that He lives! The reason for the season of Easter is to verify and confirm Jesus' fulfillment of the resurrection and His promises to us!

Jesus is also the reason Paul was chosen and blinded on the road to Damascus. He was blinded to wake him up! He was blinded so he could begin focusing on God's will for him and so he would stop persecuting Christian followers. Jesus is the reason each disciple was called from his humble lifestyle of the moment so each could follow and learn from Jesus, and then reach out and teach new followers. This caused others to believe in Jesus and to bring them to a better life and eventually to eternal life!

Jesus is also the reason Peter denied Him 3 times in an effort to save his own skin. And then when Jesus was resurrected and ate with the disciples on the seashore, Peter was the reason Jesus asked them 3 times if they loved Him. When they answered yes, He asked them to (1) feed his lambs, (2) to care for his sheep, and then (3) to feed his sheep. He was implying that we start out as little lambs, like little children, and we need to be led and fed and nurtured and taught the ways of God. Then, as we become mature and reach adulthood, we may understand things better, but we still need to be tended to, to be fed and nurtured to keep us on the right path.

Now, in addition to Jesus being the reason for <u>all</u> the seasons, we are the reason God chose to send His Son Jesus to earth to live and experience all that WE experience. We are the reason Jesus lived the life He did and why He chose to go to the cross. We are the reason Jesus was resurrected, but He is the reason for ALL the seasons – and the reason that life goes on!

"He has shown kindness by giving you rain from heaven and crops
in their seasons; he provides you with plen-
ty of food and fills your hearts with joy."
Acts 14:17

Spring

Lord,

Even though the calendar says it is too early to be spring, we are enjoying some unseasonably warm weather and there are signs that things are changing for the better around us. To celebrate, I took a walk today and found many others doing the same thing. Everyone seemed to be drinking in the beauty around us.

I passed a young couple pushing a stroller. The youngster was wearing a hooded sweater and squinting, squealing and smiling. The thought came to be that this child was seeing the outdoors – and spring –for the very first time! This was the child's first look at all that I see EVERY spring and take so for granted! For the remainder of my walk, I looked with "new eyes" at the buds, the bulbs, and the blooms all eagerly pushing their way into new life. That child is new life too, and more evidence that life goes on, season after season.

Thank You, Father, for opening my eyes to this beauty around me and forgive me for ever taking such things for granted. Help me to always feel this excited about the wonders you perform day by day.

When I consider your heavens, the work of your fin-
gers, the moon and the stars,
which you have set in place, what is man that you are mindful of him,
the son of man that you care for him?
Psalm 8:3-4

Good Advice
From a Tree

§

Books and magazines are filled with advice on how to change your appearance and become more beautiful, inside and out. Every make-up manufacturer touts his products as the best, and many are helpful in one way or another. God, too, has some practical advice for us on living our best lives and being the best we can be. For starters, He suggests that we always be ourselves, and we should always remember that each of us is a child of God

1. STAND TALL & PROUD
You are a Child of God! You are the son or daughter of a King!
You don't have to be the <u>tall</u>est, but be proud of yourself always!

2. GO OUT ON A LIMB ONCE IN A WHILE
It helps you to take some nice deep breaths & to concentrate and think.

3. REMEMBER YOUR ROOTS
They help to define you and to encourage you in each and every endeavor.
Then step out in faith!

4. DRINK PLENTY OF WATER
It's good for your body <u>and</u> it nourishes your soul!

5. BE CONTENT WITH YOUR NATURAL BEAUTY
Love who you are instead of who you <u>might</u> be!
Above all, be yourself!

6. ENJOY THE VIEW

Look around you at all the beauty nature provides and at how beautifully
things change from one season to another when the time is right!
Enjoy these changes - and above all, don't forget to look **UP**!!

Instruct a wise man and he will be wiser still;
teach a righteous man and he will add to his learning.
Proverbs 9:9

Leaving a Wake --
Making Waves

———— § ————

THE DICTIONARY SAYS that a wake is the track left in the water by a moving boat or ship. My Bible Concordance explains it as a moving ridge or swell on water. Waves can rock a boat gently on calm waters, or rock it severely during storms of any kind.

Wake-creating waves rocked the boat on the Sea of Galilee when Jesus was sleeping during a storm. Wake-creating waves carried Noah's ark along on top of the water until the rains stopped. Wake-creating waves rolled back the Red Sea so Moses and the Israelites could cross to safety.

While we live here on earth, we experience different kinds of wakes throughout our lifetime – and in all we do, we are always leaving a wake behind us. The waves we make when we create our wake affect everyone around us and every family member coming after us. In a way, we are always setting an example... When things go along smoothly, the wake is there, but it is not a disturbing wake. It just creates a sort of path that shows we've been there. When our lives are in turmoil, the wake increases, and again, it affects all those around us. Our BIG wakes create smaller wakes rippling and branching out in every direction to all whose lives we touch. There are small and big wakes. Some are straight and barely noticeable while others can zig-zag all over the place leaving a very "choppy" path where it is easy to lose your balance – easy to trip and fall – easy to even drown.

Abundant Sonshine

Take a little time to talk with God about your wake. He has great plans for you and the wake in your life. He's a wonderful, compassionate listener, and besides, He has all the answers!!

Let the righteous rejoice in the Lord and take refuge in Him;
Let the upright in heart praise him!
Psalm 64:10

He stilled the storm to a whisper; the waves of the sea were hushed.
They were glad when it grew calm, and he guid-
ed them to their desired haven.
Psalm 127:29,30

Hands

JESUS' HANDS WERE <u>never</u> still. He never stood around with His hands in His pockets. He was constantly reaching out to people to fulfill their needs. He used His hands to touch and to heal. He used his hands to form the spittle he put on a blind man's eyes so he might see. He used them to caress the little children lovingly as they came to him. His hands were often folded in prayer and supplication, as they were at Gethsemane before his arrest. They were used to heal the arresting soldier's severed ear – and then they were harshly nailed to a cross.

There are many references to hands throughout the Bible. In Isaiah 53 the prophet refers to Jesus and his <u>wounded</u> hands. John 13 tells of Jesus washing the feet of the disciples with <u>humble</u> hands. I Timothy refers to <u>holy</u> hands. Luke 22 tells of <u>grace-giving</u> hands as Jesus shared communion with his disciples. Some of Jesus' last words on the cross were about the hands of God as he said, *"Father, into your hands I commit my spirit."* Later the Risen Christ told the disciples to see his <u>pierced</u> hands and feet so they would know the truth of His resurrection.

In thinking of Jesus' hands and the many ways He used them, we can see how important our hands should be in service to Him. Our hands can be open flat – or cupped – they can grasp or they can hug – they can wave or they can clutch, either in fear or in love – or they can be folded in prayer. When we fold our hands to pray our thoughts turn to God. We don't have to fold them to pray, but by folding them it helps to close out the world and then we can concentrate and focus on Him.

Years ago there was a television commercial that showed two sets of hands and asked the viewer to tell which hands belonged to the mother and which belonged to the daughter. If you close your eyes, can you picture the hands of your parents? Picture your mother's hands as she bathed you as an infant, as she held you on her lap and read to you, as she cooked, or ironed your clothes. Then picture your father's hands as he worked in the yard, and as he hammered and sawed pieces of wood to make a doll house or as he assembled a wagon or a bicycle. Then picture his hand as he reached for your hand to cross a street or a parking lot.

How do your children and grandchildren picture YOUR hands? How do others see your hands? More importantly, how is Jesus seeing your hands? Is He going to have to ask you how you used them to serve Him? Or will He already know?

The works of his hands are faithful and just;
all his precepts are trustworthy.
Psalm 111:7

Enough

———— ◊ ————

THE WORD "ENOUGH" was used several times in a sermon at church not long ago and it prompted me to really think about that word. The dictionary says it is "as much as or as many as is desirable, tolerable, sufficient, etc." When I looked in my Bible Concordance I was surprised to see how many times that simple word appears in the Bible.

In Proverbs enough appears at least two times. In Chapter 11 it implies that he who has enough gains even more by sharing what he has with those in need. Verse 25 says this: *"A generous man will prosper; he who refreshes others will himself be refreshed or rewarded."* Later, in Chapter 28 verse 18 we read that a man whose walk (or life) is blameless is kept safe but those whose ways are improper or wicked will suddenly fall.

Another Concordance listing for enough refers us to Psalm 24. This Psalm is often referred to as the Reigning Shepherd's Psalm. It reminds us that the earth is the Lord's and so is everything in it because He made it. We are urged to have clean hands and a pure heart and we are encouraged not to turn to idols or be led by the false teachings of those who would try to tempt us. The Psalm closes with reminders that the Lord Almighty is the King of Glory and we are challenged to open our hearts and invite him into our hearts and our lives. Having God as our champion is all we need! It is enough!

In I Corinthians 9 Paul speaks of his reward in preaching the gospel. He says he offers it for free because his reward comes in seeing lives changed as people's hearts are opened in acceptance of what God offers to believers. He says his blessing comes by realizing he has been faithful to Christ in preaching, by hearing the Lord say "Well done!" and of seeing others happily coming to a life with Christ.

Enough. When is enough enough? This question makes me think of several verses in Matthew Chapter 25. In this chapter Jesus is talking with the disciples in parables. Starting with v. 34 it says, *"Then the King will say to those on his right, 'Come, you who are blessed by my Father, take your inheritance, the kingdom prepared for you since the creation of the world. For I was hungry and you gave me something to eat. I was thirsty and you gave me something to drink, I was a stranger and you invited me in, I needed clothes and you clothed me, I was sick and you looked after me, I was in prison and you came to visit me.' Then the righteous will answer him, 'Lord, when did we see you hungry and feed you, or thirsty and give you something to drink? When did we see you a stranger and invite you in, or needing clothes and clothe you? When did we see you sick or in prison and go to visit you?' The King will reply, 'I tell you the truth, whatever you did for one of the least of these brothers of mine, you did for me.'"* Later in the chapter, in vs. 45 & 46 Jesus concluded with these words: *"The king will say, 'I tell you the truth, whatever you did not do for one of the least of these, you did not do for me.' Then they will go away to eternal punishment, but the righteous to eternal life."*

These verses can be summed up this way: Rewards in the kingdom of heaven are given to those who serve without thought of reward. There is no hint of merit here, for God gives out of grace, not out of debt. Enough may never actually *be* enough. But it is enough that we try, if we try *hard* enough.

Compassion

———— ❦ ————

THE WORD COMPASSION combines the Latin words "together" and "to suffer." To be compassionate is to have feelings or sympathy <u>with</u> someone – to feel their hurts and to suffer with them. It expresses sorrow in their time of need – and you cannot feel compassion without also feeling a desire to help. From the very beginnings of His ministry, Jesus' compassion was constantly demonstrated and evidences of His compassion were always followed with action.

The story of the woman at the well in Samaria appears in the 4th chapter of John. The Jews and Samaritans had no dealings with each other. In fact, they went to great lengths to avoid each other, but as the woman approached the well where Jesus was resting, He asked her to draw Him a drink. She was surprised at His request but she was respectful, calling Him "sir." He knew all about her before their conversation began, but He asked questions to draw her out. He helped her recognize her sinful ways and past mistakes – and then He took them away from her! He unburdened her! He cleansed her and offered her the Water of Life! He knew she was carrying a burden of sin, and He had compassion on her as an individual.

In Mark, Chapter 5, Jairus, one of the synagogue rulers, came to Jesus and fell at His feet pleading with Him to heal his 12 year-old daughter who was dying. Jesus accompanied him to his home and was told the girl had died. Jesus took her by the hand and she stood and walked! But look! He did not stop there! He not only took care of the <u>big</u> things, he also saw to the small details, because He asked them to give the girl something to eat! This was compassion shown to an entire family!

Jesus had just been told His beloved friend John the Baptist had been killed in Matthew 14. He tried to go away to a solitary place to mourn but the crowds followed Him on foot from several surrounding towns. The crowds gathered near Him and "When Jesus landed and saw a large crowd, he had compassion on them and healed their sick" (v.14). But again, that was not the end of it! Later that afternoon He fed them all! Five thousand men plus women and children! That was compassion shown to the multitudes!

Lastly, let's look at Luke 10 and the story of the Good Samaritan. A man was attacked by robbers, stripped of his clothes, beaten and left half dead in the road. Several people ignored him as they passed by, but the Good Samaritan stopped! He took pity on him, he nursed his wounds and then carried him to a neighboring house and even left money to cover the cost of his care. (Notice he did not leave his name and phone number in hopes of a reward!) He left knowing the stranger was recovering. He had compassion on a total stranger! He got involved! But again, the story does not end here. Luke 10:37 is both a command and a challenge because Jesus says, *"Go and do likewise!"*

These examples show different types of compassion. We read about compassion to one person, to a whole family, to a large crowd, and to a complete stranger. Think back in your own life to times when a friend, or perhaps even a stranger, showed compassion when you needed it. You don't have to have the gift of healing to be compassionate! Just hugging someone who is hurting or grieving is a form of compassion. Caring for a sick child or an elderly parent can be viewed as acts of compassion. We are told to love the Lord first and our neighbors as ourselves. In Hebrews 13:16, Jesus said, *"And do not forget to do good and to share with others, for with such sacrifices God is pleased."*

Let's allow compassion to become a part of our daily walk with God. After all, God had enough compassion for us to send His son to die for us. Let's hope <u>we</u> have enough compassion to live for Him!

Because of the Lord's great love, we are not consumed,
for his compassions never fail. They are new every morning;
great is your faithfulness.
Lamentations 3:22-23

More of God's Gifts to Us

A is for Anger, which should be treated carefully and directed appropriately.

B is for the Breath of life. Take a nice deep one right now and thank him for it!

C is for Choices. <u>C</u>hrist <u>H</u>elps <u>O</u>ur <u>I</u>deals <u>C</u>enter on <u>E</u>ternity.

D is for His Divine protection.

E is for Eternal Life with Him in heaven when our earthly life comes to a close.

F is for Forgiveness – and Family – and Fellowship.

G is for Glasses to improve our vision – Bless the eye doctors and lens makers!

H is for Hope. Where would we be without it!

I is for the Inspiration we receive when we soak up His Words from the Bible.

J is for Joy - and it comes in SO many forms.

K is for Knowledge, something we can never have too much of!

L is for Love - the ability to give it, to receive it and to demonstrate it.

M is for Memory – and Mind – and Mountaintop experiences, all of which help us work our way through the deep valleys.

N is for the North star for guidance – and how nice that we have to look UP to find it!

O is for Opportunities – for worship and education; to help others come to know God.

P is for Prayer. Aloud or silent, anytime and anywhere.

Q is for Quiet, and for calming and inward reflection.

R is for Roots. They help to secure us and help us grow in the right direction.
S is for Seasons, both in our lives and in our surroundings.
T is for our Tears, which may blur our vision temporarily, but they also cleanse.
U is for Uplifting experiences.
V is for Valley experiences, which help us appreciate the mountaintop experiences.
W is for Words. God's infallible Words for our comfort and for our well-being.
X is for (e)Xamples by which to live.
Y is for Yoke. When we yoke ourselves to Him, he shares the weight of our problems & eases our burdens.

Z is for Zeal and Zest to keep us moving forward.

Friends

—— ∮ ——

FRIENDS. JUST THINKING about our friends can often make us smile. There are many kinds of friends: old friends, new friends, best friends, true friends. In your lifetime you will have thousands of acquaintances, hundreds of colleagues, and dozens of neighbors, but very few true friends. Don't confuse a casual friendship with a true friend. Your best friends – your true friends – will level with you, even at the risk of alienating you for a while. More importantly, your best friends will criticize you privately and they will encourage you publicly. Remember, it is better to select friends based on their character and not on their compliments.

A writer once said that true friends are never acquired by chance; they are always gifts from God. Another writer wrote, "A friend is a person whose face lights up with a sparkling glow when you walk into a room." To have good friends is one of the highest delights of life; and to BE a friend can be one of the noblest and most difficult and challenging of undertakings!

It's fairly easy to make new friends – and almost impossible to make old ones. Friends truly are a gift from God. He gives us people who love us unconditionally – or who love us *anyway*, or *just because*. Having friends makes us friendlier – even to those we may not consider close friends. A friend will share our burdens and multiply our joys. A friend is one who does his knocking before he enters instead of after he leaves… Remember, quality counts far more than quantity in terms of friendship.

The word "friend" is a word Jesus used in His last talk with the disciples. In John 15 when they were all together in the Upper Room for the Last Supper, these were Jesus' words:

"Greater love has no one than this, that he lay down his life for his friends. You are my friends if you do what I command. I no longer call you servants, because a servant does not know his master's business. Instead, I have called you friends, for everything that I learned from my Father I have made known to you. You did not choose me, but I chose you and appointed you to go and bear fruit – fruit that will last. Then the Father will give you whatever you ask in my name. This is my command: Love each other."

In the Living Bible, Proverbs 27:19 says this: *"A mirror reflects a man's face, but what he is really like is shown by the kind of friends he chooses."* Take time often to thank God for your friends. Then consider taking time to call them to thank them for being a friend. Lastly, pray for them and for your mutual friendship.

Perfume and incense bring joy to the heart,
and the pleasantness of one's friend springs from his earnest counsel.
Proverbs 27:9

Numbers

Have you noticed that numbers are directing our lives more and more every day? We have numbers for our houses, telephones in our homes and now cell numbers too. We have numbers for social security, for credit cards and zip codes. Our cars have license and engine numbers and many of us have pin numbers, and now there's also talk of our birth order numbers! Our schools have numbers for grade levels and some school systems use numbers to explain the performance levels of students. Some people think they have lucky numbers! The calendar consists of numbers of months and then the months are numbered by days. The monetary systems of the world are all made up of numbers. My family genealogy requires that each person I record has a number so they can be filed with the right family and right generation. We cannot get away from numbers!

In Biblical times, numbers were very important too. The fourth book of the Bible is called Numbers. This Book presents an account of the 38 year period of Israel's wandering in the desert following the establishment of the covenant of Sinai. In this book, the Lord spoke to Moses and told him he was to take a census of the whole Israelite community by their clans and families. Every man aged twenty years or more and able to serve in an army was to be listed, one by one. They were to be listed by name and they were to be numbered. The Lord gave Moses one name from each tribe who was to be appointed to help. Please remember there was no paper back then or an endless supply of pens or pencils, and no computers on which to record this information. Can you just imagine how huge a task this was?

They called the community together and did as the Lord asked. The smallest tribe, Manasseh, had 32,200 members. The largest was the Tribe of Judah with of 74,600 members. When they had completed this task they came up with a total of 603,550 registered names. This was not ALL of them. Remember, they only listed men aged twenty years or more who were able to serve in the army. The members of the Tribe of Levi were counted last and in their case, all over the age of one month old were numbered, and they totaled 22,000. They were not to be counted with the others because the Tribe of Levi was assigned to be in charge of the Tabernacle of the Testimony rather than be recruited for to serve in the army. This group responsibility would be to care for the Tabernacle and to move it when necessary.

When the Tabernacle was finally erected, all the tribes camped around it. The Levites were to camp in the middle and the twelve tribes were divided into groups of three as they camped around the Tabernacle with the rest of their tribe. 186,400 camped facing east, 151,450 camped facing south, 108,000 camped facing west and 157,600 camped facing north.

Today, let's remember that no matter how the world looks at us, in God's eyes we are important! We truly are more than just a number to Him. Each of us matters – you might even say that we are each number one in His eyes! He is concerned with the old and the young, with the male and the female. He wants what is best for each of us, and He wants our devotion and our dedication. But most of all, remember that He wants to be #1 in our lives!

Search me, O God, and know my heart; test
me and know my anxious thoughts.
Psalm 139:23

The Curtain

—— § ——

SOON AFTER MOVING to another state years ago, I was invited to join in a weekly Bible study program. The group had been studying the Book of John for some time and they were now studying and learning about the crucifixion. I was just awed each week as the Lecturer spoke at length about different Bible stories and passages and when she talked about all that was happening to Jesus at the time he hung on the cross and died I was deeply moved by all of the signs and the prophesies fulfilled through his death. I was familiar with the happenings, but never having really studied the Bible in depth, I did not know these details.

One part of what I learned stands out in my mind even today are these verses in Matthew 27:56 and 57: *"And when Jesus had cried out again in a loud voice, he gave up his spirit. At that moment the curtain of the temple was torn in two from top to bottom. The earth shook and the rocks split."* The mental picture that those words conveyed to me was simply astounding! Torn in two from top to bottom! Mark 15:38 says, *"The curtain of the temple was torn in two from top to bottom,"* and in Luke 23:45 it says, *"the sun stopped shining and the curtain of the temple was torn in two."*

The Lecturer then spoke at length about that phrase, "the curtain." She also gave some facts about it and how it came to be. In Exodus we learned that this veil or curtain was made by divine command. It was to separate the Holy Place from the Most Holy Place in the Temple. It was also called a "shielding curtain" because it shielded the Ark of the Covenant. We all know what a shield does – it protects. This curtain was to shield or protect the Ark from any or all who might come into its presence.

The directions and specifications of this veil were very precise. They were in cubits but I have transferred them – as best I can – into feet so we can better picture it. The veil or curtain was to be 45 feet long and 6 feet wide. There were to be two sets of five and each group was to have 50 loops so they would face opposite each other and there were to be 50 gold clasps to fasten them all as one unit. This curtain was to be made of blue, purple and crimson yarn and fine linen with cherubim sewn into it. It was to hang on gold hooks on 5 posts of acacia wood that were overlaid with gold, and each post had a bronze base. Hearing these measurements, are you getting some idea of how *very* large and how *very* heavy this veil would have been? NO one could have torn that curtain from top to bottom but God Himself!

Let's go back to those verses in Matthew 27 again. *"And when Jesus had cried out again in a loud voice, He gave up his spirit. At that moment the curtain of the temple was torn in two from top to bottom."* What was above that curtain? God Himself! What was below that curtain? We the people! Now that veil, or shield, had been removed! Christ's death opened the way straight up to God! Now it was possible for all believers to go directly into God's presence!

Paul wrote these words in Hebrews 10:19-23: *"Therefore, brothers, since we have confidence to enter the Most Holy Place by the blood of Jesus, by a new and living way opened for us through the curtain, that is, his body, and since we have a great priest over the house of God, let us draw nearer to God with a sincere heart in full assurance of faith, having our hearts sprinkled to cleanse us from a guilty conscience and having our bodies washed with pure water.*

Let us hold unswervingly to the hope we profess for he who promised is faithful."

How fortunate we are that God created this way for us to come directly to Him -- and how fortunate we are that Jesus was willing to sacrifice Himself on the cross to accomplish this end.

Rejoice in the Lord, you who are righteous, and praise his holy name.
Psalm 97:12

Leaves

---§---

OH, LORD, THERE are <u>more</u> leaves out there! I raked and raked yesterday and had them all gathered and bagged – and today there are more all over the ground!

Thank You for the leaves, dear Lord. They are a reminder that You are near and nature is going on and on whether we are ready or not. Seasons and leaves come and go. They sprout and grow and then they fall and wither and are gathered up.

Thank You for their protective greenery during the warm summers and for the shade they provide and the gentle rustling noises as winds breeze through them. And thank You for taking them away for a while. Then we can see the sky more clearly – then we can see clear up to You if we try!

Thank You, too, for the promise of new growth in the spring when buds form. I'll gladly rake again, Lord. It makes me feel You and I are working together! And while I'm raking those leaves, Lord, help me to do some "raking" in my personal life, too. Help me to gather up some of my old habits and sinful ways so I can stuff them into the bags with the dead leaves!

He has shown kindness by giving you rain from heaven
And crops in their seasons; he provides you with plenty of food
And fills your hearts with joy.
Acts 14:17

Abundant Sonshine

As long as the earth endures, seedtime and harvest, cold and heat,
summer and winter, day and night will never cease.
Genesis 8:22

Salt

——— § ———

BASICALLY SPEAKING, SALT is a seasoning and also a preservative used against decay. To be effective, salt must be pure. Salt can be sprinkled on and rubbed in, and too much of it can damage that to which it is applied. In the chemical world it is referred to as sodium chloride. It is white and it is found in natural beds underground or in the sea. Salt can also be used to slow down the degenerative process. It can be used to season food, cure meat, preserve fish, and it was also rubbed on infants years ago to cleanse them and assure good health. In Bible times, a covenant sealed with salt was considered unbreakable and the two parties ate the salt to show their good faith. It was often regarded as more valuable than gold and it was occasionally used as an exchange, or bartered for goods.

In Biblical times, salt came from great distances. It was carried on the backs of camels in long caravans along very dangerous routes. Since there was not a lot of it, it was used very carefully. It was expensive but people paid the price because no one could do without it. It was essential to purify, to preserve and to flavor food. There were no refrigerators in those days, and no tin cans or sealed packaging. In fact, there often wasn't very much food! Without salt, there might have been starvation.

Actually, through the ages salt has had many functions. It maintains health, preserves, seasons, heals, symbolizes loyalty and friendship in the form of a covenant, and it was used in the offering of sacrifices. So it has purity, preservation abilities and flavor. To penetrate, salt must be applied. To permeate, it must be present. To perform, it must impregnate.

Salt also penetrates. If you put a pinch into a jug of water, all the water becomes salty. It permeates and diffuses its way into every drop in the jug and once it is IN the jug, it cannot be taken out again. Salt also sterilizes and cleanses. It counteracts decay, deters decomposition, and it purifies and prevents undue pollution.

In Matthew 5:13 Jesus said, *"You are the salt of the earth."* Jesus asked his followers to permeate and penetrate society. Let's remember that salt is not showy – it is not decorative – it is simple and it is silent – and it is sensitive to the Spirit of God. He also calls us to "lose ourselves" in Him, just as salt loses itself in a sacrifice in the Old Testament or in healing. Let's use the salt shakers on our tables or in our kitchens to remind us that, as Christ's followers, we are to be the salt of the earth. Let's remember, too, that if we are to be the salt which penetrates society spreading word of God's love and the serenity and unity we can only get from Him, we must demonstrate these qualities. We cannot give to others what we do not have ourselves. With God's help, we can season the lives of all with whom we come in contact as we continue sharing the Good News.

Lastly, salt makes you thirsty. To be "salt" means you keep wanting more and more, and God never quenches that thirst for Him!

"Salt is good, but if it loses its saltiness, how can you make it salty again?
Have salt in yourselves, and be at peace with each other."
Mark 10:50

Going and Going and . . . . .

———— ∮ ————

Happiness keeps you SWEET …

Trials make you STRONG …

Sorrows keep you HUMAN …

Failures make you HUMBLE …

Success keeps you GLOWING …

BUT ONLY GOD CAN KEEP YOU GOING!

Where to Find Help
in the Psalms

—————— § ——————

For Comfort	Psalm 23…73:25-28…102:1-12&19…200…130
During Disappointment	Psalm 55…62:1-18
Depressed – Discouraged	Psalm 16…34…42…43:5…55:22-23…103:1-6
Doubt	Psalm 8…146
Fear	Psalm 23…27…46…91
Finances	Psalm 37:16&25-29…49:10-13&20
Growing Old	Psalm 37:23…19
God's Guidance	Psalm 15…23…73:23-26
Guilt	Psalm 19:12-14…103:8-19
Help	Psalm 5…46…57…86…121…142
Hope	Psalm 25:21…31:23-24
Joy	Psalm 30:4-5&11-12
Patience	Psalm 13…37:1-10…40-1-5
Praise	Psalm 47…100…145…147…150
Pride	Psalm 131
Erase Rejection	Psalm 38
Rest	Psalm 91
Retirement	Psalm 90…145
Sick or Suffering	Psalm 31:9-10…109:21-31…119:153-160…121
Need Strength	Psalm 46…138
During Temptation	Psalm 19:12-14…141

Reasons to Trust in God	Psalm 3:5-6...25...31:1-5...37:3-6...46:1-3...112...143
Overcome Worry	Psalm 25...112:1-8

Made in the USA
Lexington, KY
17 September 2017